Mystery
on the Vineyard

Mystery

on the Vineyard

POLITICS, PASSION AND
SCANDAL ON EAST CHOP

THOMAS DRESSER

Charleston   London

THE
History
PRESS

Published by The History Press
Charleston, SC 29403
www.historypress.net

Copyright © 2008 by Thomas Dresser
All rights reserved

Cover design by Marshall Hudson.

First published 2008
Second printing 2008

Manufactured in the United States

ISBN 978.1.59629.423.3

Library of Congress Cataloging-in-Publication Data

Dresser, Tom.
Mystery on the Vineyard : politics, passion, and scandal on East Chop / Tom Dresser.
p. cm.
ISBN 978-1-59629-423-3
1. Murder--Massachusetts--Case studies. 2. Murder--Massachusetts--Martha's Vineyard-
-History--20th century. 3. Martha's Vineyard (Mass.)--History--20th century. 4. Martha's
Vineyard (Mass.)--Biography. 5. Rice, Ralph Huntingdon, b. 1886--Trials, litigation, etc.
6. Trials (Murder)--Massachusetts--Martha's Vineyard. 7. Acquittals--Massachusetts--
Martha's Vineyard. 8. Smith, Clara M., d. 1940. 9. Murder victims--Massachusetts--
Martha's Vineyard--Biography. I. Title.
HV6533.M4D74 2008
364.152'3092--dc22

2007052326

In memory of John Morelli,
an inspirational Vineyard teacher and friend;
Ruth Hughes, who first broke the story in the press;
Bernie Cournoyer, my esteemed father-in-law;
and John Walter, editor and co-publisher of Vineyard Stories.

CONTENTS

FOREWORD

Tom Dresser's work is an excellent example of the symbiotic relationships that exist between archives and writers. While part of our mission at the museum is to collect and preserve material, it is only when the information that has been preserved is made available to the public that we fully accomplish that mission. Thanks to Tom's sustained and careful efforts, this fascinating story will now be known by many and the material in our archives has truly helped this part of the island's past to be part of the present and the future.

Matthew Stackpole
Executive Director, Martha's Vineyard Museum
Edgartown, MA
November 26, 2007

As the newspaper of record for Martha's Vineyard for 161 years, the *Vineyard Gazette* is a rich repository of history and long-running journal of the life of an Island situated seven miles off the southeastern coast of Massachusetts. An author who delves deeply into the *Gazette* files will find all sorts of untold tales, and Tom Dresser did exactly that as he researched the story of the Rice School murder.

Julia Wells
Editor, *Vineyard Gazette*
Edgartown, MA
December 4, 2007

PREFACE

Every town has its skeletons, ghosts and embarrassing past. Every so often one of these tales slithers out from beneath the closet door to be reviewed and revived in the light of day.

This story happened on East Chop in Oak Bluffs nearly seventy years ago, on the cusp of the Second World War. It was the dawn of the summer of 1940. In that sepia-toned era, the Red Sox led the American League in early June and John Steinbeck's *Grapes of Wrath* had recently been released as a movie, starring Henry Fonda.

On the northern tip of Martha's Vineyard, just seven miles off the southern arm of Cape Cod, Oak Bluffs, with a population of fifteen hundred, prided itself on its staid Methodist campground, the Baptist Highlands and a small Christian Science community nestled between the two. The Rice Playhouse was a cultural enclave in Oak Bluffs, where Broadway actors performed summer stock shows. At the adjacent Rice School of the Spoken Word, instructors taught elocution or proper speaking techniques with a Christian Science bias.

Circuit Avenue hosted a honky-tonk, post-Prohibitionist fervor. It was a brazen time, but not a dangerous one. Houses were left unlocked, crime was negligible and Vineyarders all knew one another.

Americans were about to reelect Franklin Delano Roosevelt to an unprecedented third term. The president had drawn the economy out of the Great Depression and was prepared to deal with the European conflict. Isolationism was in vogue, although a cocky Hitler strolled through Paris, which was vanquished like much of Europe. England was next.

The brutal robbery, rape and murder of an elderly widow shocked the summer community and drew the rapt attention of the East Coast press.

Yet to this day, the crime is still listed as unsolved. Not only was a woman viciously murdered, but her killer was never apprehended.

The Rice School murder has lingered for generations in the shadows of memories, yellowed newspaper clippings and tawdry folklore. This is the story of that crime and the injustices it spawned.

ACKNOWLEDGEMENTS

I want to express appreciation to those people who helped me on my way. It was a treat to meet Bill Talley and the wonderful people in Vanceburg, Kentucky, from the Lewis County Historical Society to the Victorian Rose.

Research led from Vanceburg to Hammond, Indiana, to Grand Junction, Colorado, and back to New Bedford, Massachusetts. I made internet friends all along the way. The amiable abilities of researchers and librarians are to be commended. My thanks to Betty Caseman, Bill T. Clark, Robert W. Cresse Jr., Shelia Heflin, Molly Herron, Shirley Hinton, Patty Kennard, Patricia Kincaid, Michael Menard and Ann Marie Tomascik.

Of course, on the Vineyard many people pitched in. My thanks to Sue Canha, Jim Cummings, Tom Dunlop, Bob and Ruth Hughes, Rick Kelley, Mike McCormack, Phylis Meras, Michael O'Keefe, Bob Penney, Art Railton, Eulalie Regan, Joe Sollitto, Matt Stackpole, Peter VanTassel, Liza and Tim Williamson and Linda Wilson. And I want to credit Cynthia Riggs, author of a half-dozen Vineyard mysteries, who first alerted me to the tale of "the beautiful young actress" who was slain on the Vineyard shores.

My personal editor, John Hough, added a great deal to the finished product. I want to thank our old writing group—Mike Ditchfield, Maureen Hall, Molly Hitchings, Brenda Horrigan, Ann Lees, Shawn McCormack, Eric Shenholm and Jim Venuto—and my new writing comrade, Maureen Hourihan. Also, Don Bracken and Richard Maurer each encouraged my efforts.

Bob Aldrin rose from his sickbed to edit the images. I am indebted to him for his dedication to high-quality product.

I especially want to thank my editors at The History Press, Saunders Robinson and Hilary McCullough, who kept me focused on the goal of a well-prepared book, and Dani McGrath, who has been super in sales and promotion.

The story lives on. With the devastating fire at the Bunch of Grapes bookstore in July 2008, we count on Edgartown Books, gift shops and libraries to share the story.

Susan Canha, granddaughter of Phidelah and Elizabeth Rice, says, "It's time the story was told. Too bad Mother didn't live long enough to see this very positive book." Barbara Cottle Child recalls Carolee Rice always "liked to be quiet about the murder."

One woman told me her husband was the first Oak Bluffs police officer on the crime scene; another recalls her parents owned property by the Playhouse. Jessica Andrews, of Tucson and Oak Bluffs, noted that her father, Basil Langton, once ran the Rice Playhouse.

Valerie Sonnenthal suggested we advertise for the missing front page of the *New Bedford Standard Times*. Kristen Kingsbury Henshaw questioned why the judge ignored the obvious involvement of Harold Tracy. An Oak Bluffs senior asked if we should track Tracy's descendants.

Prior to publication of *Mystery on the Vineyard*, Tom Dunlop analyzed the murder in *Martha's Vineyard Magazine*. In high school, Sarah Greenberg and Kara Rosenthal filmed *An Unsolved Mystery*, a fine video based on this story. Corinne Kurtz plans to use the trial in her Martha's Vineyard Regional High School history class. These efforts keep the story alive.

Work is underway on a website, thomasdresser.com.

When the final word is written, however, it all comes down to my wife Joyce, who deserves unending credit. She shared in my exhilaration and worked me through my frustrations. Her unwavering support and encouragement kept me on track, and together we made it. Many thanks, Joycie!

chapter one
JUNE 30,1940

An intruder slunk through the unlocked screen door into Sumner Hall. He walked across the common room, past the great stone fireplace and then slowly took the stairs to the second floor of the dormitory. He pushed open the first door at the top of the stairs, room fifteen, where Clara Smith slept soundly. The intruder closed the door behind him. What happened next is based on conjecture, on the condition of the room and the earwitness accounts of two dozen women who slept in the dormitory that evening.

He attacked her. That the intruder raped Clara was proven by semen found on her body. She scratched at him, plucking hairs from his head. As he committed his violent deed, the intruder clamped his hand over her mouth. Her cries were muffled, indistinguishable moans and groans.

"At the time I thought of it as being a nightmare," her companion Pearl Blakeney later recalled. "Like someone trying to talk and couldn't. It sounds as though someone may have taken their shoe and hit on the wall or the floor with the heel of it."

Blood splattered the wall and floor. The wastebasket and bedside table were knocked over. Sheets were yanked off the bed. Books were scattered across the floor.

The intruder struck Clara on the head with a sharp object, the edge of a board or spine of a book. That blow fractured her skull. Then he put his hands around her neck and strangled her. Whether it was the shock of the violent rape, the blows to her head or the stranglehold on her neck, Clara Smith died within minutes of the attack.

The intruder made off with her ring and gold watch. A few girls in the dormitory stirred in their sleep, but no one saw or heard him leave the premises.

An eerie sense of calm settled over the dormitory. The girls fell back asleep.

Settled as a missionary outpost in the 1640s to convert native Wampanoag, Martha's Vineyard blossomed with the whaling industry for a century and a half. As whaling waned with the Civil War, oil was discovered at Titusville, Pennsylvania, in 1859, and the electric light bulb was invented in 1879, agriculture took hold. In many ways the Vineyard remained a remote seaside refuge, apart from the bustle of mainland activities. In 1940, the population of Dukes County, which includes Martha's Vineyard and the Elizabeth Islands, hovered around five thousand people.

When one visits the Vineyard by boat, the first identifiable structure is the East Chop lighthouse, which stands on a headland, high enough to serve as a signal site before the arrival of the telegraph and telephone. Semaphore flags signaled a whaling ship's return. From Woods Hole, on the southern shore of Cape Cod, to Telegraph Hill on East Chop, from East Chop to Cape Poge on the western shore of the island of Chappaquiddick, and on to Nantucket, signal flags were hoisted by captains who wanted their families and backers to prepare for a great return, or at least to alert them they were on their way home after months, even years, at sea.

East Chop earned its name from the choppy tidal waters around the headland. West Chop, a sister peninsula, also features a lighthouse, and together the two spits create Vineyard Haven Harbor. This harbor, which runs nearly a mile inland, became a maritime mecca in the nineteenth century, when great three-masters would put in for supplies, repairs or to entice sailors aboard. In fierce storms as many as two hundred sailing ships would seek shelter in the harbor. Vineyard Haven became an integral port on the commercial route for ships that sailed through Vineyard Sound between Boston and New York in the eighteenth and nineteenth centuries.

East Chop Drive runs around the Chop, past the towering, shimmering lighthouse and the impressive shingled summer estates high on the cliffs and then curves gracefully down along the harbor and into town. Less than a half mile from the lighthouse was the Rice School of the Spoken Word and the Rice Playhouse, a cultural cluster in Oak Bluffs. Several of the buildings enjoyed panoramic views of Vineyard Sound, facing east, into the rising sun. Highland Wharf was close by the school, with the town pier around the harbor. The school owned a beach wagon to transport

Since the 1880s this was known as the Chocolate Lighthouse for its reddish brown color. East Chop light was repainted a bright white in the 1980s. Its license from the U.S. Coast Guard is maintained by the Martha's Vineyard Museum, which recently refurbished it. *Photo by the author.*

students to the steamships that ferried passengers and autos across the sound to Woods Hole in Falmouth. The beach wagon made many trips that June weekend in 1940 to pick up students, actors, employees and Rice family members. It was a busy time of year for the school, indeed, for the entire populace of Martha's Vineyard as they readied their island for the influx of summer visitors.

The Rice School campus sprawled across the lower end of East Chop with four dormitories for the summer students and actors. Work was underway to spruce up the playhouse for July 1, opening night. New personnel had to be hired and trained, housed and fed, directed and supervised. Returning employees and students served as mentors for the newcomers and united the body of students, faculty and players.

The Rice family had to deal with a critical issue that summer. Phidelah Rice, the family patriarch and founder of the Rice School and the Playhouse, was not in good health. For decades he had been a progressive director, manager and nationally known actor, but Rice fell ill to an undisclosed illness that spring and arrived on the island on June 28 in a weakened condition, unable to assume the responsibilities of his school or the playhouse. His unmarried elder sister May took over management of the school, with the assistance of Phidelah's wife, Elizabeth Pooler Rice.

That the Rice family were strong adherents to Christian Science precluded any medical intervention for Phidelah's condition. Christian Scientists believe the patient would be healed by praying for a better understanding of God's spirituality rather than seeking medical assistance.

The playhouse was leased to a pair of men already involved in management of the Rice operations, Charles Cook and Paul Whitney, when it became apparent that Phidelah could no longer function as director. The torch was passed.

Yet even with Rice's absence in overseeing activities on the campus, life appeared to be moving along, more or less on schedule.

Clara M. Smith was a short, obese woman, reputedly wealthy, who originally came from Conshohocken, Pennsylvania, a suburb of Philadelphia on the Schuylkill River. She lived at 6 Regina Road, Dorchester. For twenty years, she and her late husband William had been readers in the Second Church of Christ Scientist.

Clara had never been to Martha's Vineyard before. She arrived on June 12 for a vacation-education at the Rice School and was met at the boat by the school secretary, Lydia Kipp. Handyman Jan Thomas drove her in the beach wagon to Sumner Hall, the shingled school dormitory right on the shore, then carried her bags upstairs to room fifteen.

Pearl Ella Blakeney resided at 11 Ocean Street, less than a mile from Mrs. Smith, down Washington Street, also in Dorchester. She was a Western Union file clerk, born in Canada, who had attended the Rice School the previous two summers. It was at her urging that Clara joined her for the summer term.

The women had registered for a two-week diction class that consisted of a dozen hour-long sessions. Twenty-four students were enrolled in the school that term. The school brochure described the diction class as one that included "correct breathing, vocal support, breath control, vocal placing and the education of the tongue, lips and jaw in correct vowel formation and consonantal articulation." Board was eighteen dollars per week and tuition amounted to forty dollars for the two-week program.

On her first and only trip to Martha's Vineyard, dowager Clara Smith met an untimely demise in Sumner Hall. *Courtesy of the* New Bedford Standard Times.

From the 1940 brochure, this shot of the Club House and Sumner Hall epitomizes the weather-shingled dormitories Rice School students were required to board in during the summer term. *Courtesy of the Martha's Vineyard Museum.*

Clara and Pearl had met a decade earlier through the Christian Science Church in Dorchester. Clara was seventy-two and Pearl only thirty-two. They were both devout Christian Scientists. At the Rice School, their instructor, Ralph Huntingdon Rice, younger brother of Phidelah, described Clara as one who took her religion very seriously. She "talked about it too much," he said. Pearl ministered to Clara's medical needs, which included a weak heart and shortness of breath. They viewed their time on the Vineyard as a healthy vacation.

They sat together in the crowded dining hall that Saturday evening amid fellow students and playhouse employees. The frankfurters, beans, brown bread and coleslaw were typical Saturday night fare. For dessert they enjoyed strawberry shortcake, as local berries were just coming into season.

By six o'clock on that warm June evening, the dining hall was full of anticipation. Those students of the Rice School of the Spoken Word who had just completed their first semester enjoyed a break between terms. For others, actors and set builders who worked for the Rice Playhouse, this was a time to gear up for the opening performance of the eight-week summer season. Thespians took a break in the preparation of the production of *A Bill of Divorcement*. Coincidentally, a movie of the same name was screened that same weekend, in the same town, a quarter mile away in downtown Oak Bluffs.

With their classes over, Clara and Pearl planned to travel together to Nantucket, a sister island to the Vineyard, some seventeen miles off the Cape. They were booked on the morning boat, which was scheduled to arrive in Nantucket before noon. They dawdled over dinner, not wanting the evening to end. Around 7:30 p.m., the two women left the dining hall to pass through French doors and stroll along the verandah to soak up the salt air in the lingering sunlight.

Later they sat in the community room and watched other residents. At nine o'clock Clara said she still had a few more items to pack. Slowly they ascended the wide staircase in the center of Sumner Hall. They said goodnight at the top of the stairs, and Clara opened the door to room fifteen, while Pearl proceeded down the hall to room fourteen. It was dark outside now, and the dormitory quieted down, though an occasional student disturbed the silence by opening the side door and taking stealthy steps on the stairs.

Pearl read for a while, finished her packing and then went to bed between 10:00 and 10:15 p.m. The soft splash of a wave against the shore was comforting. Night air flowed through the room. A car muttered down East Chop Drive and into town.

Clara piled her Christian Science books neatly together on her bedside table. She packed her clothes in a large satchel, but left her slip on the chair, a paper clipped to one strap with fifteen dollars wrapped inside. She removed the screen and opened the window to allow the soft breeze in. Then she slipped into her nightclothes, pulled the cord on the light over her bed and fell asleep.

After midnight the back door slapped when a couple of latecomers returned. Marjorie Massow came in the side door and went up to her room on the third floor. She and her roommate Ruella Robertson had been to the movies with a couple of boys from the school. The girls talked in their room for a while, and then Ruella fell asleep. Marjorie wrote a couple of letters, did her nails and then went downstairs for a glass of ice water in the cooler in the dining room. When she tiptoed back upstairs, it was after 1:30 a.m.

The women on the second and third floors slept soundly. It was sometime after two o'clock in the morning. The night sky was lit by the meek waning moon. This was the coolest time, the darkest time, the quietest time of night.

The sky gradually lightened and pinked, and a brilliant sun gradually rose from the ocean horizon. The sweet scent of beach roses permeated the air. It was going to be a gorgeous day.

Breakfast was served at 8:00 a.m. Pearl and Clara always waited for each other. Pearl sat patiently, awaiting her traveling companion. She thought perhaps Clara still had packing to prepare for their departure. Perhaps Clara had overslept. Pearl went upstairs to wake her.

She paused for a moment outside room fifteen, listening. Only an eerie silence greeted her. Pearl knocked. No response. She knocked again. Then she opened the door. It was a little after eight o'clock on the morning of Sunday, June 30, 1940.

chapter two
TWO ISLAND INSTITUTIONS

With the Vineyard separated from the mainland by miles of ocean, an insular mentality evolved and locals looked within for motivation and leadership.

Over the years the Rice Playhouse grew into a cultural treasure that summer visitors were quite proud of. And the *Vineyard Gazette* offered a social conscience for the Island, a sense of justice and fair play. These two institutions proved a source of pride, and each was dominated by a prominent individual.

THE RICE SCHOOL AND PLAYHOUSE

Phidelah Rice was born May 4, 1881, in Grand Junction, Colorado, the fourth child of Phidelah and Annie Rice. Although his father was a rugged westerner in the lumber and cattle business, early on, young Phidelah showed promise on the stage. He recalled being mesmerized at a performance of *The Merchant of Venice* as a boy. To his father's chagrin, he won a public speaking prize, which earned him the attention of the superintendent of schools, who advised the senior Rice to advocate acting as a career for his son. "What have I done that a boy of mine should want to go on the stage?" his father wondered.

Phidelah began his professional career at the Leland Powers School in Boston. As student and later teacher, he was there for sixteen years. It was there he met Elizabeth Pooler, who became his wife. Together they founded the Rice School of the Spoken Word in 1912.

The school began inauspiciously with four students at Trinity Chapel in the Wesleyan Grove in Oak Bluffs, but quickly outgrew the confines of that site. In 1914, the Rices purchased acreage on East Chop, on the southern side of the Highlands. This area was once a prominent Baptist community but by then was a maze of dirt roads that interlaced the woods and fields of East Chop.

Phidelah Rice attained national acclaim from a unique form of acting. He assumed several characters in a popular play, in succession, playing one role after another. Monacting was defined as the reading or acting of a play by a single actor.

Phidelah believed people of each community should have the opportunity to attend theatre, as he had as a youth. In 1924, he and Elizabeth opened the Rice Playhouse, the second summer theatre in the nation. They grew it into a viable island establishment, a premier playhouse.

Phidelah was master of both school and playhouse. He read with sincerity, beauty and power and perfected his craft over a twenty-year career. He was avidly sought in lecture and lyceum settings across the country.

The Rices wintered in Brookline, Massachusetts, but in summer he was the theatrical maven on the Vineyard. The Phidelah Rice Players were known as a distinctive repertory team.

The Rice Playhouse produced notable Broadway plays of the caliber of the 1925 Pulitzer Prize–winner *Hell-Bent-Fer-Heaven* and *A Bill of Divorcement*. Phidelah brought the works of Noel Coward to the Vineyard and was eager to promote new theatrical ventures each year.

The Rice Playhouse was a cultural oasis amid the warren of dirt roads on East Chop. Broadway stars performed here from 1924 through 1940. *Courtesy of Jane Meleney Coe,* A Guide to East Chop Families, *2002; used with permission.*

In 1930, Phidelah toured from Maine to the Deep South to promote himself and his playhouse. He enticed Broadway star Jessie Rogers to perform on the Vineyard stage. One of her early leads was in *The More the Merrier* in its world premier on the Vineyard.

While the country suffered through the Great Depression, the Rice Playhouse staged premier plays in its small summer theatre. Often the two-hundred-seat theatre was sold-out. The playhouse was truly a community center, with paintings and pottery on display in the lounge for the enjoyment of the audience, musical recitals to entertain playgoers at intermission and soft iced drinks available at a refreshment stand.[1]

To further boost attendance, Rice arranged free bus service from the Island House on Circuit Avenue, with stops at the Wesley Hotel and Ocean View Hotel. An evening ticket was $1.50 while a program of nine plays, with front-row seats, cost $12. Reservations could be made at the pharmacies, or by dialing the three-digit exchange "551". The playhouse proved profitable.

Publicist Rose Rosner Cook wrote a weekly playbill. Her words embodied the spirit Phidelah Rice sought to convey, that the arts bring hope in dire times, such as the Depression. Cook elaborately described playhouse happenings and extolled Phidelah, from his charming personality to his sincerity as both artist and man.

In 1932, Phidelah opened a twenty-five-seat children's theatre, with two plays each season. Phidelah was often seen with his white mane flowing dramatically as he hurried through a children's production or dashed into a rehearsal. Over the years he introduced Vineyard children and summer people to the stage in shows from the memorable *Peter Rabbit* and *Little Joan of Arc* to *Treasure Island.*[2]

In its ninth season, Phidelah arranged a benefit for the Vineyard branch of the Animal Rescue League. He was drawn to Kitty Foote and her efforts to protect animals on the Vineyard. He helped her cause and promoted his playhouse at the same time.

Phidelah brought Emily Post to lecture on inhabiting the role each actor assumes, which depends on understanding how the character must feel. As in her dictates on etiquette, she said, "We must have the rules, because they make for ease, for smoothness." Another year Mrs. Leland Powers spoke on the import of public speaking.

And it was not just the playhouse that blossomed. When the Rice School of the Spoken Word observed its silver anniversary in 1936, it was considered the country's premier school on elocution. Phidelah's younger brother, Ralph Huntingdon Rice, was on the faculty, with a résumé that stated he had been a student of voice production and a professional singer

"Broadway on the Island"

THE ISLAND PLAYGOER

Published Weekly by the Phidelah Rice Playhouse
at East Chop, Martha's Vineyard, Mass.

Vol. 2, No. 1.   Edited by Charles Emerson Cook   July 1, 1933
Publicity Director

PHIDELAH RICE
Director Rice Players and Theatre Workshop

Playhouse founder Phidelah Rice struck a dignified pose on *The Island Playgoer*. Rice was known nationwide for his acting prowess. *Courtesy of the Martha's Vineyard Museum.*

This 1932 brochure contained a syllabus of classes, including diction, public reading, extemporaneous speech and expressive movement. Theatre classes ranged from speaking voice, costuming and philosophy of expression to scene building and painting. *Courtesy of the Martha's Vineyard Museum.*

for twenty years. The campus boasted a dozen classrooms, four dormitories, a studio, a workshop, a successful theatre and an enrollment of more than two hundred students and teachers.

Yet Phidelah sought national acclaim. In the off-season, he and Elizabeth cultivated a large following in the Midwest. Their public readings and workshops proved popular, and they incorporated new ideas into their summer programs. At the Cleveland Playhouse, Phidelah gave a six-week performance in which he estimated twenty thousand people heard him perform as the bishop in *The Bishop Misbehaves*. He was so proud he wrote a letter to Henry Beetle Hough of the *Vineyard Gazette*, and enclosed clippings of his record-setting performance.

A *New York Times* review praised Phidelah's role in New York in *Hamlet*. He "played twenty-five characters and, it seemed, was not even close to exhausting his resources. He walked around one side of a chair, for instance, as Polonius, reappeared on the other side as Hamlet, sat down and recited a soliloquy."

The *New York Post* raved that Phidelah Rice was an amazingly gifted actor. The *Christian Science Monitor* said he held his audience spellbound. The *New York Sun* considered him the country's most eminent monactor.

All this adulation was not lost on Rose Cook. She proudly recapitulated the comments for the benefit of the Oak Bluffs audience in her weekly playbills and characterized the playhouse as "Broadway on the Island."

When Rose's husband Charles Cook, along with Paul Whitney, assumed management of the theatre in the summer of 1940, due to Phidelah's failing health, they replaced the first eleven rows in the theatre with new leather seats and planned to extend the playhouse season by one more week for a total of nine weeks. They also raised ticket prices from $1.50 to $1.65, and the Wednesday matinee increased a dime, to $0.75. All signs pointed to a prosperous summer season.

The playhouse opened with *A Bill of Divorcement* on Monday, July 1, 1940.

THE VINEYARD GAZETTE

Henry Beetle Hough received a wedding present he cherished all his life. His father gave him the weekly newspaper, the *Vineyard Gazette*, when he and his wife settled on Martha's Vineyard in 1920.

Henry Hough grew up in the seafaring town of New Bedford, on the shores of Buzzards Bay. New Bedford, like Nantucket and Edgartown, had been a dominant whaling community in the nineteenth century. When whaling ebbed, the economy shifted to cotton mills and New Bedford flourished as a textile metropolis. But the mills moved to the South in the early years of the twentieth century, due to the availability of cheaper labor, and since then New Bedford has languished.

Hough's father was city editor of the *New Bedford Evening Standard*. In 1898, when Henry was two years old, the senior Hough purchased property in North Tisbury, so Henry and his older brother George summered on the Vineyard's north shore, in a house called Fish Hook.

Hough went to the Columbia University School of Journalism, class of 1918. Like Phidelah Rice, he met his future wife in school. Both women were well educated and were devoted to their husbands' career paths. And both were named Elizabeth.

At the time of their wedding, the Houghs faced stiff competition from two rival newspapers. The *Gazette* circulated among a meager six hundred residents. The Houghs set out to turn their paper around. Early on, the Houghs bought out their competition, the *Martha's Vineyard Herald* and the *News of Vineyard Haven*, which gave the *Gazette* a monopoly of the island press.

Over the course of half a century, the *Gazette* came to be recognized for its dedication to causes, from saving trees on State Road to articles that supported Kitty Foote and the fledgling Animal Rescue League. The Houghs devoted themselves to the preservation of their idyllic island community. Their journalistic style ranged from specific personal stories to advocacy of public issues such as ferry service to the Vineyard.

In 1928, the Houghs built a house in Edgartown, a short bicycle ride from their busy office. Betty loved her garden, which provided a sanctuary from the rigors of editing the weekly paper. When they needed to get out of town, they drove fifteen miles across the island to Fish Hook to enjoy a respite from the relentless challenges of their chosen career.[3]

In 1929, the Houghs purchased a Duplex press for $6,500, capable of printing on two sides of the page at once and folding the paper. That summer they initiated printing on Tuesday as well as Friday, to meet the needs of summer people and gather increased advertising revenue. The summer tradition continues today.

Hough managed the linotype and publishing functions of the paper, and often penned the editorials. He also wrote books. He published the first of twenty-seven books in 1936, entitled *Martha's Vineyard: Summer Resort, 1835–1935*. By printing only two thousand copies, he broke even. Two of his best-known efforts, which brought national recognition, were *Country Editor* (1940) and *Once More the Thunderer* (1950).

A fire at the *Gazette* office in 1935 forced the Houghs to publish across the water. Henry's brother George had followed their father's journalistic path and served as editor and publisher of the *Falmouth Enterprise*. He helped his

The *Vineyard Gazette*, founded in 1846, was edited for more than half a century by Henry Beetle Hough. The *Gazette* moved into these offices the year before the murder. *Photo by Bob Aldrin.*

younger brother out. By the spring of 1939, the Houghs found a new office, on Summer Street in Edgartown, and the *Gazette* moved into the historic building it occupies to this day.

As whaling died out in New Bedford, it did so in Edgartown as well. The town and much of the island welcomed tourists and summer visitors. Hough advocated improvements in island transportation, until he realized such plans would lead to a loss of island identity. When state highway engineers sought to make the Vineyard conform to Commonwealth standards with wider roads and broader bridges, Hough fought back.

Two issues exemplify Hough's stance against state interference in Vineyard roadways. He argued against cutting eighteen trees and widening the bridge at the old ford in North Tisbury. Later, when the highway department advised the town to chop trees on Middle Line Road for improved visibility, the *Gazette* stood firm in support of the rural nature of the island and against standardization of roads. Hough succeeded in both ventures.[4]

Following the 1938 hurricane, Hough opposed state bureaucrats who sought to replace the damaged Edgartown lighthouse with a stark metal frame with a beacon at the top, more of a light tower than a lighthouse. Hough insisted that Edgartown harbor, home of the whaling industry, required a picturesque lighthouse. He led the move to purchase a used lighthouse from the North Shore town of Ipswich and have it barged to Edgartown, where it sits today.

In the lead-up to World War II, Hough hesitated to cover world affairs, casting the *Gazette* as a bastion of local journalism. Yet as parochial issues became entangled in the World War, he resigned himself to report on the conflict as it impacted his Vineyard audience.

As the *Gazette* reported that late June of 1940, Hough was optimistic about the upcoming season. Although the weather had been damp and dreary, he expected it would be a glorious summer.

The grisly murder of Mrs. Clara Smith rattled the island and shook the very souls of these two influential, intellectual leaders of Vineyard cultural institutions. It fell on the shoulders of the editor of the *Vineyard Gazette* and the owner of the Rice Playhouse to support the police in their pursuit of the criminal who had so violently disrupted the serenity and security of the island. In their own ways, Henry Beetle Hough and the Rice family sought to restore normalcy to the summer, but their task was almost insurmountable.

chapter three

THE LONGEST WEEK

Hearing nothing, Pearl opened the unlocked door and looked about the room. "I removed the blanket from the pillow," she said, "not really expecting to see her there. I thought perhaps she had stole a march on me and gone down ahead of me."

Pearl stared down at the bludgeoned face and beaten body of her companion. She dashed downstairs to notify the housemother, May Rice. In a frightened voice she said she thought Clara Smith had died of heart failure.

May Rice summoned Dr. Francis Buckley, who arrived shortly after 8:30 a.m. He pronounced Clara Smith dead, due to a hemorrhage. Later he qualified his statement that the "cause of death is that Clara Smith died of extensive injuries to the brain within thirty minutes of the attack." The body was stiff; rigor mortis had already set in.

Dr. Buckley telephoned Oak Bluffs Chief of Police Gus Amaral, but he was marching in a parade, though he did show up later that morning to make a cursory examination of the crime site, leaving fingerprints throughout the room. Amaral had the presence of mind to notify the state police and call in a police photographer, who duly photographed the crime scene before the body was removed to the Martha's Vineyard Funeral Home.

From the moment she realized Clara Smith had been murdered, May Rice concealed the tragedy from her students. "When I first met her," said Dr. Buckley, "she seemed quite interested in having me keep the thing as quiet as possible, due to the fact that there were many young girls in the house and it would be prejudicial to their existence to have a scandal, or a panic, or whatever you might call it."

Furthermore, May Rice decreed that police were to dress in plain clothes so as not to arouse suspicion. She spread a rumor that motion pictures

umner Hall buildings at East p, Martha's Vineyard, scene of death of Mrs. Clara P. Smith, of Dorchester. Mrs. Smith's body, with skull crushed and body battered, was found in a bedroom on the second floor over the piazza of the white cottage. The cottage contains kitchen, dining room and bedroom facilities. Sumne Hall proper is the two-story build ing at the right.

The Club House (left) served as dining hall for the two dozen female students who bunked in Sumner Hall. *Courtesy of the* New Bedford Standard Times.

were being taken on the campus, hence the photographers. "Excitement at the school was kept at a minimum," the *Gazette* reported, "most of the students knowing nothing of what had happened until an announcement was made."

Ruth Hughes of Oak Bluffs broke the story in the news media. She recalled,

> *Nick Altieri from the State Police came to our house, actually Bob's parents house over on Pequot Avenue. We were having dinner. He said, "Ruth, I have a scoop for you. There's been a murder." My paper* [New Bedford Standard Times] *was the first with the news. I went to the room at Sumner Hall. There was blood on the wall. I was kind of scared, with all the cops around, but it was part of my work.*

"In those days," said her husband Bob, "Ruth got paid ten cents an inch for her stories. This article was such big news they gave her a $5 bonus."[5]

Ruth filed her story ahead of the Vineyard, Boston and New York papers, which chased the *Standard Times* for the lurid drama.

"You know they [*New Bedford Standard Times*] couldn't afford a photographer," Bob Hughes said, "so they asked me to take pictures. I had an old bellows camera, folds in and out, but I didn't have a flash. So I asked this buddy,

Larry Goldberg of the *Boston Post,* to stand beside me. He set off his flash and I took the picture. It worked out all right." Bob also assisted by calling in a story for the *Boston Herald.*

He added, "It's all we talked about. There was talk about getting locks for the doors, but we never even had a key."

News of the murder traveled rapidly across the Vineyard.[6]

Chief Augustus Amaral was a local boxer of some renown who used to fight Hector Benefit of Edgartown. Initially he took charge of the investigation, but quickly turned authority over to the state police. The state police were headquartered in the Dr. Tucker house, the decorative structure with the raised red roof that overlooks Ocean Park. Assistant District Attorney Edward Harrington was "summoned at once and reached the Island on the late boat Sunday," according to the *Vineyard Gazette* of July 2.

The *Gazette* reported, "District Attorney Crossley made a flying trip from New Hampshire." He met with state police officials and physicians already on the island. A state pathologist and fingerprint expert were summoned.

In the autopsy Dr. Buckley performed the next day, he described how Mrs. Smith was savagely beaten with a dull object about her head. In concise terms the medical examiner said, "C.M. Smith died as a result of the application of blunt violence to the head with resulting injury to the brain...homicidal assault." Prior to the murder, Dr. Buckley concluded, "My opinion is she was ravished. Intercourse (was) involuntary." Initial reports indicated knife wounds to the abdomen, but these were revised to scrapes inflicted by sharp fingernails. An effort was made to strangle her; fingernail marks were etched in her neck.

No detail in the autopsy was omitted. Mrs. Smith's hair was gray, tinged with brown, of average texture and appeared to have been waved. "The hair was enclosed in a coarse hair net and there were several curlers on each side." Time of death was estimated to be six hours before the body was found, based on partially digested cabbage in her stomach. "The mouth had no teeth." In Mrs. Smith's right hand was clenched a single human hair.

As far as motive, the initial assumption was robbery. "The impression was gained that the bruising of the left ring finger was such as might be expected to occur if a tightly fitting ring had been forcibly removed," said Dr. Buckley. Missing were a diamond ring and a white gold watch.

Assistant District Attorney Edward J. Harrington released particulars of the stolen items, which were broadcast on the radio. The wedding ring was a twin setting, fourteen-carat gold, chromium plated, with three-quarter-carat diamonds, with a carved orange blossom on each stem. The Waltham watch was also fourteen-carat gold, a square Tonneau timepiece with rounded corners. It had fifteen movements. Serial numbers were listed.

The *Morning Mercury* of New Bedford led with the story, with a dateline of June 30. "State and local authorities tonight were preparing to launch a full-scale investigation into the death of Mrs. Clara Smith, who was found, her skull battered and her body gashed, in her quarters at a Sumner rooming house today."

The *Mercury*, the *Gazette*, the *Standard Times*, the *Cape Cod Times*, the *Boston Post* and the New York papers featured the story, although the *New York Times* buried the piece, "Woman Beaten to Death," on page fourteen.

Donald Billings was nine years old in 1940 when he went door-to-door delivering the *Standard Times*. The area around Sumner Hall was roped off on that morning, he recalled. Mr. Billings said his parents spoke quite a bit about the murder at the dinner table.

Islanders who scanned the front page of that Tuesday's *Gazette* read a piece on an additional steamboat run added to the schedule to accommodate the anticipated influx of visitors for the Fourth of July celebration. The *Gazette* predicted, "All signs point to a summer business at least as good as that of last year." Plans were finalized for the parade in Edgartown.

Another story, more somber in tone, reported more than seven hundred pounds of donated clothing were collected for the British War Relief Society and packed into two dozen cartons to be shipped to England in support of the British resistance against Hitler's impending attack. German U-boats had already attacked merchant ships in the Atlantic. The war was getting close.

The big news, of course, was the murder. In eighteen-pica type the *Gazette* blared, "Homicide is Expert Verdict as Elderly Woman is Found Dead in Dormitory Room." In italicized headlines, the *Gazette* recounted that the victim was a seventy-two-year-old woman who had intended to leave the island the day her body was discovered. The story was all in bold type. State and local police were on the trail of the criminal. Once the reader waded through the headlines, what else was there to say?

District Attorney William C. Crossley of the Southern District released a statement to the press: "That the cause of death was injury to the brain, due to fracture of the skull; that death had been almost instantaneous, the victim having breathed no more than twice following the blow; that there were marks on the throat but not sufficiently in evidence as to signify strangulation; and that the victim had been criminally assaulted."

The violent scene in room fifteen was described in detail. State police assumed the intruder came inside Sumner Hall and up the stairs, rather than scaling the wall and entering through the open window, "because the nature of the crime suggested a narcotic addict or a sex maniac who would have been more likely to enter the ground floor."

The *Gazette* morgue was a maze of newspapers, but has since been organized, with 150 years of *Gazette*s neatly boxed. *Photo by the author.*

The district attorney tried to run the investigation, but had to leave the island to give a speech. He was running for attorney general of the Commonwealth and had his political obligations. It was expected he would return the next day. Further investigation was underway and state police officials announced that "the traditional police dragnet is spread."

In an effort to capture the suspect, boats were watched. Dry cleaning establishments were warned to report any bloodstained articles of clothing.

On the same front page that described the murder, an advertisement announced, *"A Bill of Divorcement*, not a picture, not a shadow substitute, but played by a living cast of Broadway's finest actors." The star was Joanna Roos, a Broadway actress who often appeared in summer stock. Miss Roos performed in both San Diego and the New York Shakespeare Festivals, and later appeared in films and the soap opera *Love of Life*. The ad implied the show at the Rice Playhouse would go on, murder or not.

Forty-four-year-old, gray-haired Clarence Lester Smith, a foreman at the Kerite Company in Seymour, Connecticut, arranged for his stepmother's body to be brought back to Dorchester. The son had been scheduled to meet Pearl and Clara on their return from the islands. Reporters noted, rather obviously, that "the circumstances deeply concern him." When he had last seen his mother, he said, she was eagerly anticipating her vacation.

Mrs. Smith was only the sixth murder victim in the three hundred years of island history. Two murders occurred in the late 1600s; both victims were Indian squaws. Another Indian woman was killed in Gay Head in 1823, and forty years later, the *Gazette* morgue read, "One William C. Luce of Vineyard Haven was done to death violently in his store, but the murderer was never apprehended."

The most recent homicide occurred in 1935 on the shores of Lake Tashmoo in Vineyard Haven. The gunman, Harold Look, suffered delusions that Knight Owen was interfering in the life of a woman Look felt responsible for. Owen, quite drunk, sat in his car while Look fired four shots, killing him on the spot. Look was found insane and sentenced to Bridgewater State Hospital.

The *Gazette* commented that when the criminal is captured, "as Islanders feel sure he will be," he would be tried on island. The article went on, "There is no precedent in modern times for a murder trial in this county."

Until 1935, Nantucket and Dukes County did not try capital cases, due to an 1832 law that required transfer of such cases to Bristol County. The legislature revised that statute in 1935, cognizant that travel off island caused hardship in lost time and wasted expenses. The murder trial would thus be the first held on Martha's Vineyard.

State police questioned the men associated with the Rice businesses. One of them, Ralph Huntingdon Rice, was interrogated by the police on Wednesday afternoon. At first Huntingdon refused to speak with the officers, as he was on his way to an appointment. He was convinced, however, to meet with police, and described to them how he first heard of the crime.

> *It was the next day after it happened* [Monday, July 1]. *I was coming over here* [Sumner Hall]—*I have to drink buttermilk before I retire to help me sleep, and I was coming over here to get some buttermilk. She* [his sister, May Rice] *said the woman* [Mrs. Smith] *had died and they thought from a heart attack and you people* [the police] *thought from murder. That is all I know about it.*

The Fourth of July dawned wet and windy, yet the *Gazette* cheerfully reported, "Edgartown paraded on the Fourth, paraded with martial music, colors flying, and a festive air throughout its long line of march, despite the rain." Another account noted someone fired off firecrackers, even in the midst of a downpour. The weather was quite dreary. "One scarcely needs official confirmation of the all too evident fact that the weather this spring and early summer has been sadly lacking in warmth," the *Gazette* intoned.

By Friday, July 5, homeowners' nerves were on edge. In Oak Bluffs, an unidentified intruder tried to get into the house of Mr. and Mrs. Cooper Gilkes. Mrs. Gilkes's screams scared off the would-be invader. The *Gazette* reported that "Chief of Police Augustus F. Amaral lost his temper in a manner quite foreign to that officer, as he branded the story as hooey." It was revealed, upon further investigation by the police, that the "intruder" was a motorist who had run out of gas and went house to house looking for the owner of Wormley's service station.

Hardware stores sold out their supply of locks. Houses that had not been secured in generations were fitted with new clasps and bolts. More than two hundred locks were installed in the houses of Oak Bluffs that early summer.

The district attorney had a state chemist flown over to the island to join the pathologist and fingerprint expert.

Twenty-two-year-old Elmer Keyes of Boston was arrested and jailed in Edgartown for larceny of less than $100, specifically two pairs of women's silk stockings. Though not a suspect in the murder, he acted suspiciously when questioned by police as he was preparing to leave the island. He was held on $200 bail.

Jan Thomas, a handyman from Kentucky employed by the Rice Playhouse for the summer, was arrested on charges of possession of a concealed weapon. He was not linked to the murder either, but was incarcerated at the Edgartown jail when he could not make the $1,000 bail.

Reporters compared notes. Friday's *Gazette* observed that "for a group of officers supposedly frustrated in their efforts, soaking wet from the heavy rain, and both hungry and tired, these men appeared to be singularly good-natured and satisfied. It was inferred from this fact that the day's work had not been without promising results." Perhaps it was wishful thinking or a hint they had their man, but the investigation apparently was drawing to a close.

Editor Hough weighed in with an editorial. He observed that the violence came at the worst possible time of the year, as it interfered with the start of the summer season. He assured his readers justice would be served. It may well have been wishful thinking on his part as well, or an effort to calm his public, but Hough, like the officers, sounded sure the crime would soon be solved.

He added, "Meantime a special word of sympathy should be said, not only for the family of the woman who met death here, but for the Rices whose premises were violated by this one tragic lightning stroke. Their summer school was developed by devoted efforts from small beginnings,

Dr. Tucker was a patent medicine physician at the turn of the twentieth century. President Ulysses Grant stayed here during his Vineyard visit in 1874; the building housed the state police in the 1940s. It is currently used for condominiums. *Courtesy of Bob Aldrin.*

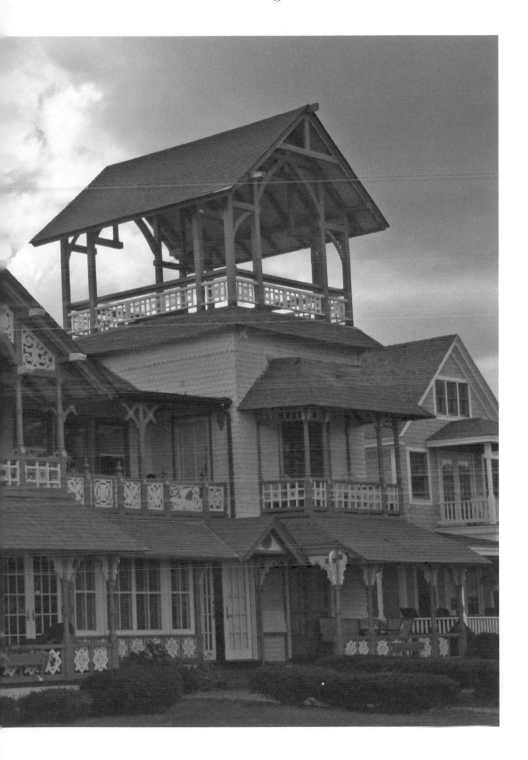

over a long period of years, and it has an honorable record. It has come, too, to mean a great deal in the summer life of the Vineyard." Hough recognized that the murderer killed not only Mrs. Smith, but also destroyed the sanctity of the Island. "The peace and protection which they [visitors] seek on the Island is one of the important elements of life."

Huntingdon Rice returned from downtown on Saturday evening, July 6, after mailing a letter at the post office. A playhouse sign had been knocked over and he ran ahead to the theatre to report the damage to manager Charles Cook. Huntingdon said the sign was probably knocked down by vandals. School secretary Lydia Kipp was in the box office, counting receipts from the performance of *A Bill of Divorcement*, which was then in the third act. She later stated to police that Huntingdon had a "very fearful look in his face," which frightened her. Mr. Cook invited Huntingdon to go in and watch the rest of the play, but he said he was too distraught. He couldn't watch the play because it made him sad.

The look Huntingdon shot Miss Kipp was so frightful she asked to spend the night with friends. When her friends would not accommodate her, she went to the police. They entreated Bob and Ruth Hughes to keep Miss Kipp overnight.[7]

From Kipp's report of the fearful look, the state police summoned Huntingdon for further interrogation at one o'clock on the afternoon of Sunday, July 7. He was brought to a glassed-in porch at the Dr. Tucker house, with police guard, even when he went to the bathroom. Because he missed dinner, he was offered a cheese sandwich and a glass of his beloved buttermilk.

The questioning was intense. Huntingdon sweated profusely, and the officers assumed that was further evidence of his guilt. By 6:30 p.m., Huntingdon was so wrought-up he sent a telegram off to his Christian Science practitioner, with the plaintive words: "Investigated by police since 1 pm. Suspect being framed. Feeling ill. Please help." It was already too late.[8]

Police kept the pressure on Huntingdon from 1:00 p.m. that Sunday afternoon until 3:00 a.m. the following morning. At 3:15 on Monday morning, July 8, District Attorney William Crossley arrested Ralph Huntingdon Rice and charged him with the rape and murder of Mrs. Clara Smith. Sheriff Thomas Dexter transported Huntingdon to the Edgartown jail, where he was held without bail.

chapter four

ODD MAN OUT:
RALPH HUNTINGDON RICE

R alph Huntingdon Rice was born in 1886, the youngest child of Phidelah
and Annie Rice. The other progeny were David, Mary (known as May
or Maribelle), Bernard, Phidelah and William. Huntingdon readily admitted
that as a young boy he was spoiled by his older siblings. Often it was his sister
May who took care of him. One of his favorite childhood activities was to ride
a horse around his father's ranch, carrying mail. Once he was thrown from the
horse and injured. He later claimed he never completely recovered from the
accident and the injuries sustained in that fall plagued him the rest of his life.
An operation at the age of twenty-three incapacitated him for nine years.

Huntingdon's father, Phidelah Sr., was born in Kentucky in 1845, and
shortly thereafter the family moved to Missouri. He became a Presbyterian
pastor, but contracted tuberculosis and could not maintain the rigors of
the post. In 1870, he married Annie Marcella Bernard, born and raised in
Baltimore, who had moved to Kansas City, Missouri.

Phidelah Sr. sought outdoor employment to counteract the effects of the
tuberculosis. He moved to Colorado and bought a ranch in Grand Junction
to raise and herd cattle. With the encouragement of his wife, he planted
apple trees and developed a fruit farm. He ventured into the nascent lumber
business in the early 1880s and, with his brother William, acquired a sawmill
to form Rice Brothers, a successful operation in Grand Junction. By the end
of the century, he was considered a prominent figure in western Colorado.
William's death in 1901 left Phidelah Sr. as sole proprietor.

As a minister, Phidelah Sr. occasionally officiated at weddings and
funerals and remained dedicated to his church. He was an advocate of the
Prohibition movement and ran for secretary of state.

As the youngest son of a father with such an impressive résumé, young Huntingdon struggled to emulate the successful career his father had carved out. The rest of the Rice children followed their father's trail with varying degrees of success. As a woman, May was not encouraged to go to college or seek a prominent position. For decades she labored for Phidelah Jr. at the Rice School.

David, the eldest son, died at the tender age of ten in 1884, and William Ormel Rice died at twenty-two in 1904, so neither son had to prove himself before his father.

Bernard graduated from Colorado College, then attended theological seminary at Tennessee's Cumberland University. He was instrumental in the creation of the Westminster Foundation, a key financial arm of the Presbyterian Church.

In 1904, Phidelah Jr. also graduated from Colorado College and then made his way to the Leland Powers School of the Spoken Word in Boston. Later he launched the Rice School, and subsequently the Rice Playhouse.

Huntingdon also studied at Colorado College, but withdrew due to ill health and never graduated. He joined his father's lumber business in Grand Junction, where he worked for a number of years. He never married. The

David H. Rice, firstborn of Phidelah and Annie Rice, only lived ten years. He is buried in the cemetery in Grand Junction, Colorado. *Courtesy of Robert W. Cresse Jr.*

William O. Rice passed away at the age of twenty-two. Huntingdon was devastated by his death. *Courtesy of Robert W. Cresse Jr.*

family was protective of him, with May taking charge most often. To the family, he was Ralph or Uncle Ralph.

At age twenty-nine, Huntingdon followed his brother Phidelah to Boston to study music. To pay his way, he worked as a salesman, first at Jordan Marsh and later at Filene's. For nearly a decade he labored as a door-to-door salesman promoting electrical supplies for F.S. Hardy. But Huntingdon's true love was music, and he joined the New England Conservatory of Music, where he taught both the cello and violin.

He left Boston for New York in 1928. It was there that he sang for NBC on station WEAF and found theatre jobs in New York and New Jersey. His social life revolved around work. Huntingdon once confided to a psychiatrist that he had only three sexual encounters, all with the same aggressive woman in his apartment building in New York City. He abhorred the experience.

Huntingdon admitted he was neurotic. He suffered "nervous disability, insomnia. I overworked in New York. Sort of a nervous breakdown. I have to avoid being in crowds. I can't go to parties. In New York I can't go anywhere much. I have to lead a very secluded life. Down here it is hurly-burly, everybody after me, and it bothers me."

Anything of a violent nature caused him distress. News of the war in Europe or violent crime would upset him. "A murder committed within forty miles of me will make my hair creep," he once said, adding, "I always skip over the news accounts of such things."

Although he was endowed with a celebrated voice, Huntingdon did not often sing in public. "It was his nervousness which prevented him from winning the success to which his voice should have carried him," his brother Bernard once said. Huntingdon blamed his limited concert work on a faulty memory.

In an effort to combat his inner torments and improve social relations with those around him, Huntingdon became a student of Christian Science in the late 1920s, again following the lead of Phidelah. He contacted Edna White, a practitioner of the religion, and initiated a long-standing correspondence beginning in 1929. Over the years, Huntingdon became dependent on Miss White, who supervised a Sunday school program in New York City.

That same summer of 1929, Phidelah lured Huntingdon to the Vineyard to teach at the school, and Huntingdon returned yearly to instruct in both voice and diction. Voice was defined as the proper use of articulation, the use of the tongue, lips and jaw. He also taught students how to read the Bible aloud, in preparation for public reading, as many Christian Science students at the Rice School aspired to be readers. It was in his Bible reading class that he taught Clara Smith.

One of his students, Adelaide Bangs Urquhart, recalled Huntingdon "taught Extemporaneous Speech as well." She said the school's classrooms were at the back of the theatre. "There were two more classrooms under the stage, a rehearsal hall, and even the auditorium which were variously in use." Eight to ten students were in each class. Thus the school and playhouse overlapped in space utilization, and Huntingdon was in the midst of all the activity.

Huntingdon was named director of the department of voice at the Rice School. The *Gazette* reported he "has been successful as a teacher, and that his students have valued his instruction even when, because of a lack of diplomacy or social feeling on his part, they may not have liked him personally."

When both parents died within weeks of each other in the early 1930s, Huntingdon was devastated.

An intriguing footnote hinted he might be enticed to step back up on the stage. A Rice Playhouse playbill from the 1934 season contained this curious announcement: "On the subject of the gifted members of the Rice family, we also feel that it is good news to make known the fact that there is a possibility that Huntingdon Rice may be persuaded to give a song recital at the Rice Playhouse."

Phidelah and Annie Rice were notable progenitors of western Colorado in the latter half of the nineteenth century. *Courtesy of Robert W. Cresse Jr.*

This event was considered newsworthy because Huntingdon had a reputation for his "truly magnificent baritone." The promotion noted it "will be a rare treat to all of us. Heretofore, Mr. Rice had come to Martha's Vineyard each year simply to rest, but we feel he will be swayed by what may be called popular demand." It cannot be confirmed whether he actually took the stage to sing.

By the summer of 1940, Huntingdon, age fifty-four, characterized himself as a singer and teacher of voice culture and music. The previous year he had suffered a nervous breakdown prior to coming to the island, and he complained to his sister May of insomnia and nervousness in the spring of 1940. They had not seen each other since the previous fall. He did not want to return to the Vineyard that summer, but was convinced the school was counting on him, especially since Phidelah was too ill himself to teach.

Huntingdon reluctantly agreed to return to the Vineyard, full of trepidation exacerbated by nerves and sleeping disorders, according to reports May Rice received. He arrived in Oak Bluffs on May 31, 1940.

chapter five

THE SUMMER OF 1940

O n Tuesday, July 9, ten days after the body of Clara Smith was discovered, the *Vineyard Gazette* announced that the murderer had been apprehended. "R.H. Rice Arrested, Is Arraigned on a Charge of Murder." The newspaper noted that Huntingdon was a member of school faculty, that he was very calm upon his arrest and that he was apprehended because of a letter he wrote and mailed to a woman named Edna White in New York City. Huntingdon was held at the Dukes County Jail pending a hearing on July 18.

Oak Bluffs Police requested New York detectives track down the letter Huntingdon sent, subsequent to the murder. They also sought a package Huntingdon allegedly posted to his correspondent, which purportedly contained the stolen watch and ring. It was noted that in the letter to Edna White, Mr. Rice described the crime in great detail. This letter, then, was considered a key piece of evidence.

There was considerable appreciation voiced for the officers who had investigated the crime. "Wearied, pale and haggard, with nerves strained to the cracking point," the *Gazette* recounted. "Mr. Crossley and the officers relaxed for the first time since Monday morning when the case, declared by veteran newspapermen to be the toughest in the history of the Commonwealth, had been brought to the point of an arrest and a murder charge."

Petty thief Elmer Keyes was brought back into court to be transferred off island. His manner was decidedly cheerful, although he still faced robbery charges. It was entirely understandable, the *Gazette* noted, that "stepping out of a murder case to matters of mere robbery" would make most people more cheerful.

The article that announced the arrest of Huntingdon also introduced a new member of the cast. It was reported the district attorney was looking into the alibi of one Harold Tracy, also known as Jan Thomas, currently of Oak Bluffs, but originally from Kentucky. Mr. Tracy was arrested on July 5 and held for possession of a concealed weapon without a permit. He was incarcerated in the same jail as Rice.

While police questioned Tracy several times that week, apparently they did not suspect him in the murder. He readily answered their questions and was brought into custody and arrested, charged only with an illegal handgun. In hindsight, it seems incongruous that he was not interrogated more aggressively about the murder.

An intriguing aspect to the situation Harold Tracy found himself in was his romantic attraction to Marjorie Massow, a student of Huntingdon's who also worked as an usher in the theatre in return for her board. Tracy and Marjorie had been out to the movies at least once, and he was very interested in her. So interested, in fact, that he wrote her a long letter attesting to his loyalty and love and, intentionally or not, throwing the police off his scent as a suspect in the murder. (The letter is a masterpiece at deception, pledging Tracy's intent to respect Marjorie's virginity while acknowledging serious incriminating circumstances regarding the death of Mrs. Smith.)[9]

Tracy's address was listed as Vanceburg, a small town on the Ohio River in northeast Kentucky. He had been hired at the playhouse that summer as an electrician through the friendship of a member of the technical staff. Tracy admitted to having been arrested previously for drunkenness in Chicago.

Tracy's more serious brush with the law was committed in Hammond, Indiana, in 1933. Under the Interstate Transport of a Stolen Motor Vehicle Act, he was arrested for automobile banditry, i.e. carjacking. It was reported that "it appears that Tracy held up a man and a woman, getting nothing for his trouble since as he said later, they had 'half as much as I did myself.'" For this crime he was sentenced to ten years in the reformatory at Pendleton, Indiana. Following his parole in 1937, Tracy made his way to the Vineyard.

When he appeared in court on the weapons charge, a reporter for the *Gazette* wrote, "Tracy was well dressed and made a good appearance even after his night in jail. He is a presentable young man, rather on the thin side, and appears to be somewhat reserved." Tracy was tall and thin, rather good-looking, with wavy brown hair. He had the trace of an affected accent, which gave him the manner of a man of culture. Women were quite taken by him.

Readers of the *Gazette* that second Friday of July were informed the thermometer reached eighty degrees four times over the past week, hitting a high of eighty-six on July 10. Summer had finally arrived on the Vineyard after a damp, drab spring.

Products advertised in the *Gazette* included a 1940 Buick with a starting price of $895. An ad for Coca-Cola was submitted by the Tashmoo Springs Water Company, and Phillips Hardware sold beach umbrellas for $3.25. It was midsummer, time to enjoy a Coke in your new Buick, with the beach umbrella in the back seat.

The Red Sox slipped from first place to third after the Fourth of July, but were still ahead of the New York Yankees. Sophomore Ted Williams, named for the first President Roosevelt, dominated the Red Sox with his hitting. Detroit led the American League.

Across the Atlantic, Hitler sent his Luftwaffe over the English Channel in the first wave of bombing in the Battle of Britain. The British had the advantage of radar, which Hermann Goering considered inconsequential.

The lead story in the *Gazette*, again, however, was the murder. "Rice to Take Stand in His Own Defense," blared the headline, followed by, "Accused Man Is in Good Spirits."

Huntingdon's attorney, Frank G. Volpe of Boston, met for three hours with his client and declared he had complete confidence in his innocence. Volpe wanted Huntingdon to testify on his own behalf at the hearing scheduled for July 18 and dismissed the motive of robbery, noting Huntingdon had $1,500 in his bank account.

Volpe came to Huntingdon via the district attorney's office in Cambridge, where he had worked as an assistant. In 1935, he successfully requested five editors of the Harvard *Advocate* to resign in a free speech complaint over indecent short stories, one by Henry Miller. The controversy contributed to the claim that if a story was banned in Boston, it would promote sales.

Volpe wanted to show Huntingdon in the best possible light, so he paraded him out of his cell at the Dukes County House of Correction to meet the press. Huntingdon posed for photographs, attired in a smart brown suit, and appeared almost dapper. A mainland paper showed him adjusting his tie and combing his hair. The newspaper reported Huntingdon "was cleanly shaven, had good color, and smiled several times without evidence of strain. It is reported that he has been eating well, and that he has been getting along well despite the admitted nervousness which has characterized him for some time past."

Teachers on the school staff sent Huntingdon a letter of encouragement in facing this ordeal, and emphatically expressed their unyielding confidence in his innocence. His family stood wholeheartedly behind him.

Fitting inconspicuously into Edgartown's architecture, with white clapboards and black shutters, the only aberration is the bars on the second floor of the Dukes County Jail and House of Correction. *Courtesy of Bob Aldrin.*

Harold Tracy, aka Jan Thomas, was in a cell in the same block as Huntingdon. While the cells had foot-thick granite walls, there was an opportunity for prisoners in the same block to interact in a shared hallway.

A federal warrant had been issued to bring Tracy back to Kentucky to face charges for a crime he committed after his stint in the federal penitentiary at Pendleton. Tracy was wanted for a robbery in Owensboro, Kentucky.

The *Gazette* opined,

> *One of the ironies of the present case, provided Tracy goes back to Kentucky to face prison terms, is that he seems to have selected Martha's Vineyard as an ideal hideout. He is said to have gone to the library and looked the Island up from every standpoint. It seemed an ideal spot in summer, secluded and quiet, and far from crime and suspicion, yet here in the first few weeks of his stay he stumbled into detection and arrest.*

The *Gazette* considered Tracy a man of interest in the murder, a person with the capacity to commit the crime. The district attorney and police, however, focused exclusively on Huntingdon, because of his unusual personality and strange behavior.

When a photographer sought Harold Tracy's picture, the jailer said, "Mr. Tracy is very averse to photographs."

In his editorials that week, Henry Hough decried the lack of steamboat service for excursions out to Cuttyhunk and Gay Head. He praised standards at the Dukes County jail, but made no mention of its current occupants. And he waxed poetic on the smoky sou'wester: "The southwest wind of summer is a wind you see as well as feel, for it brings the lazy, sultry summer days, and then at night pours through the open window as unrelenting as the draft of an eternal electric fan." With a murder in its midst, the *Gazette* sought to soften the tone of the summer with a homily on island breezes.

District Attorney Crossley requested a special session of the Dukes County Grand Jury on July 17 to weigh evidence in his case against Ralph Huntingdon Rice. This meeting of the grand jury would preempt the lower court case, the continuance following Huntingdon's arrest.

When he moved the case out of district court, Crossley effectively nullified Huntingdon's chance to state his side of the case. Huntingdon was stifled, which enraged his attorney, Frank Volpe. Volpe offered to allow Huntingdon to stand before the grand jury, at which time he would waive his immunity. To deny him the right to speak, would, Volpe eloquently stated, "deprive the defendant of his right to present his side of the case, as only the government evidence is heard by the grand jury." Further, if an indictment were returned, as seemed likely, it meant Huntingdon would be jailed until late September, the earliest a jury trial could take place.

Volpe spoke adamantly on his client's behalf, but without success. Sheriff Dexter, who had worked the murder case and transported Huntingdon to jail, served grand jurors with a summons that the special session would convene on the date Crossley selected, July 17.

On a related topic, Henry Hough expressed outrage at what he deemed "Newspaper Fakery." He sounded off against those papers that thrived on inaccurate reporting. "If the profession itself would turn against those writers who twist and lie so flagrantly newspapers would have more respect in the world." Hough claimed that no interview was ever granted by Harold Tracy, yet such a story was reported in the mainland press. He urged readers to boycott those papers that foisted falsehoods on an unsuspecting public.

In an adjacent editorial, Hough noted that a number of Vineyarders sought more extensive reportage on the war overseas. He responded that the mainland dailies, delivered by steamship, reported current war news, and radio announcers read war bulletins hourly. Hough refused to publish what he labeled as secondhand reports from the international front. Instead, he sought to pepper his paper with stories that reflected what people experienced on the island, local tales, to combat war fatigue.

The July 19 *Gazette* bore an ad for *The Vinegar Tree*, the current production at the Rice Playhouse, with Jessica Rogers in the lead. Rose Cook's playbill described the play as a "merry comedy and the laugh of a lifetime." Again, the Rice family wanted the show to go on, even though the founder's brother was incarcerated on a charge of murder.

A workroom for Bundles for Britain, an affiliate of the British War Relief, was set up in a shop owned by Leo Convery on Main Street, Edgartown. Wool was provided so volunteers could knit clothes for the British, who were being bombarded by the Nazis. Readers were urged to contact Mrs. Hugh Bullock at Edgartown, telephone 85, to help out.

The new Jewish Community Center in Vineyard Haven was to be dedicated at the end of July, according to a committee of Henry Cronig, Dorothy Brickman and Irving Kligler.

S.C. Luce Jr., president of the Martha's Vineyard National Bank, rode his horse Calumet Doble to victory at the Metropolitan Speedway in Boston.

Although midsummer was one of the busiest times on the island, all the jurors responded to their summonses and arrived at the courthouse at the appointed time. Judge Edward F. Hanify oversaw deliberations of the grand jury.

District Attorney Crossley masterfully outlined his evidence as he orchestrated a parade of witnesses through the courtroom. Chief Amaral addressed the jurors. Officers from off island who assisted in the arrest testified. Captain John Stokes, head of the investigation, spent the most time being interviewed by the jurors.

Crossley brought in Miss Lydia Jane Kipp, secretary of the Rice School, and requested testimony from three young women who had heard strange, inarticulate sounds at Sumner Hall in the early morning hours of June 30. Pearl Blakeney, Martha Stingel and Joanne Sokol added their impressions to a growing body of evidence.

Crossley introduced post office employees from both Oak Bluffs and New York City to present an integral element in his case: the letter written and mailed by Huntingdon to Miss Edna White of New York.

THE ISLAND PLAYGOER

VOL. IX. NO. 3. JULY 15, 1940.

Charles Emerson Cook
By arrangement

Present

and Paul H. Whitney
with Phidelah Rice

ROBERT SHAYNE

THE VINEYARD PLAYERS

16th Season

Even with a murder on campus, playhouse managers felt "the show must go on." Robert Shayne (1900–1992) starred on Broadway and East Chop before he found his role in the *Adventures of Superman. Courtesy of the Martha's Vineyard Museum.*

Interestingly, neither the fingerprint expert nor the chemist who had been brought to the island for the investigation were invited to testify before the grand jury.

Again Volpe volunteered, indeed pleaded, to allow Huntingdon to testify. Crossley argued, curiously, that such testimony might prejudice Huntingdon's own rights against self-incrimination. Additionally, Crossley pointed out that Huntingdon's testimony would potentially turn the grand jury session into a judicial office, rather than its intended role of simply bringing charges. Volpe continued to advocate his client's desire to testify, but to no avail.

It took less than an hour for the jurors to reach their decision. They were solemn as they filed back into court and indicted Rice on two criminal counts, the rape and murder of Clara Smith.

Thus the wheels of justice rolled into place for Huntingdon to be brought to trial on the last Tuesday of September 1940 on murder charges. Crossley had done his job. In the height of his political campaign for attorney general, Crossley wanted to make sure that people across the Commonwealth were aware of his success at reaching an indictment in the Oak Bluffs murder.

Frank Volpe requested a change of venue for his client's extended incarceration. He cited a lack of exercise space at the Edgartown jail and said that Huntingdon required unique, unspecified attention. Although he had already spent over a week in jail, Huntingdon did not appear to suffer stress or ill effects from the experience. His face, his manner and his complexion appeared normal. The change of venue was denied.

Over in district court that same July 17, Judge A.L. Braley sentenced Harold Tracy to one year in the Barnstable House of Correction for possession of a concealed weapon. This was deemed a precautionary measure in case the district attorney ascertained there were ties between Tracy and the murder. In short, Crossley used the grand jury to land his big fish, Huntingdon, but if that one got away, he kept the minnow in a holding tank nearby, under lock and key. Or so he thought.

Tracy admitted his guilt in possession of a concealed weapon. Crossley shared with the court Tracy's criminal past, which explained why he had changed his name to Jan Thomas when he came to the Vineyard. Tracy feared he still might be required to serve out his sentence for the carjacking crime in Indiana.

That wasn't all. Crossley announced Tracy was listed as a fugitive from justice as a result of a $5,000 robbery at Grant's Jewelry Store in Owensboro, Kentucky, in 1937, shortly after his release from Pendleton Federal Penitentiary in Indiana. A small-time crook from out of state, obviously hiding out to avoid detection, aroused minimal suspicion. This was odd, yet still not sufficient to dissuade a stubborn district attorney from his prosecution of Huntingdon, even though the accused boasted an impressive professional résumé, had no motive to murder, rape or rob one of his students and clearly had pressing psychological problems. It made no sense.

As to Tracy's personal background, Crossley noted that he was divorced and had fathered a daughter who was being reared by his ex-wife.

Reporter Ruth Hughes managed to get into the Edgartown jail to speak with Tracy. She asked where he was the night of the murder. "He said he was drunk and didn't remember anything from that night," Ruth recalled.

As the summer wore on, press coverage of the case was maintained in the mainland press. Readers who spent their two cents on the *Boston Post* learned Huntingdon's alibi on the night of the murder was that he claimed to be "alone in his room all night in the Phidelah Rice house across the street" from the Sumner dormitory.

The *News of New York* opined, "The natives are all for Rice. They point out that he comes of excellent family, never drank, was an uncompromising puritan, could never have committed a sex atrocity."

Henry Hough weighed in with a request for a respite from the headlines that surrounded the murder. He admonished his readers to recognize that evidence alone was presented at the grand jury hearing, which naturally would lead to an indictment. Indictments were only an accusation, not a judgment. Hough urged his readers to reserve judgment until the court had a chance to provide Huntingdon with a fair trial, introduce exculpatory evidence and reach a decision by a jury of his peers.

In one of his most eloquent editorials on the subject, Hough wrote, "The blows which killed Mrs. Clara M. Smith also killed the peace and dignity which had surrounded an old established institution, the Rice School; they set in motion chains of circumstance which bathed innocent individuals in harsh publicity, and required others to undergo a test which was none of their making, from which they could hardly emerge unharmed." It was an impressive show of support for the Rice family, and underscored Hough's sense that justice had not been served in the indictment of Huntingdon.

In a letter to the editor, Carl Wonnberger said the Boston papers garbled the facts, while the *Gazette* offered a temperate and factual account of the proceedings. The writer complimented Hough for his exemplary journalism and praised freedom of the press, while advocating self-regulation by journalists themselves.

Another letter reacted to the announcement that the playhouse managers intended to cut the season short. John Barnes Holmes praised the Rice family for high standards of artistic merit and urged the theatre to remain open all season. It would make the Vineyard look bad if we could not keep our theatre open, he said, while the neighboring island of Nantucket supported its thespian organization.

An editorial in the *Falmouth Enterprise* noted the new managers of the playhouse were faced with a brutal murder on their campus, just as their season opened. The editorial acknowledged that fear gripped theatergoers, yet the show must go on. It pointed out that the playhouse management and cast had nothing to do with the murder.

George Hough, Henry's elder brother, went on to say that Phidelah Rice had been a popular advocate of the Vineyard for nearly three decades. This summer he was bedridden, too ill to even stand in his brother's defense. Past loyalties seemed to count for naught, the editor complained. The *Enterprise* wondered, "Would we blackball our summer theatre because it rented its roof from a man whose brother was accused of a crime? Could this tragedy have happened here?"

In a letter to the editor, Allen Tetlow urged Vineyarders to stand by the Rice family and persuade the managers of the playhouse not to close.

But the managers of the playhouse felt they had to end the season early because they were losing patronage. Actors were performing before fewer than forty people. Broadway actress Jessica Rogers, a star with nearly a decade of sold-out performances at the playhouse, found herself on stage before meager crowds.

All was not lost. Just as the managers were about to announce they had to close the playhouse a week earlier than planned, an anonymous donor contacted them and donated funds to keep the playhouse open for the rest of the season.[10]

Midsummer activities gradually pushed the murder off the front page. The July 23 *Gazette* led with news of an amphibian airplane crash in Vineyard Haven Harbor in which two people died. One story featured efforts to raise money to purchase an ambulance for England and another detailed the travails of a woman recently evacuated from the war zone.

As Paris fell to the Nazis, a Mrs. Carson, who owned homes in both Vineyard Haven and off the coast of France on the Isle of Jersey, became frantic with worry as her husband was captured when the Germans invaded their European island. Mr. Carson, identified as lord of the manor in Jersey, was now listed as a German prisoner. His whereabouts were unknown, the *Gazette* reported.

In a tender letter, Dionis Coffin Riggs, author of *From Off Island: The Story of My Grandmother* (1940), recalled, "Years ago there was great rivalry among the different towns on the Island, and as for anyone coming 'from off'—he was beyond the pale." She noted that the sense of distance on the Vineyard had all but disappeared since her youth, when she would spend all day riding in a horse-drawn carriage out to Gay Head with her grandmother. "So our rivalries are disappearing, and as lovers of Martha's Vineyard we can work together happily on a worthwhile Island project." Ms. Riggs went on to describe an all-island cavalcade designed to raise money in support of the American Red Cross.

The war in Europe influenced the daily lives of the people of Martha's Vineyard, as well as those all across the United States. By mid-August, the Battle of Britain was well underway German planes bombed airfields and factories across Britain. Fierce air battles raged in the skies. The Royal Air Force appeared on the brink of defeat, which would bring Britain to its knees.

Hitler declared a blockade of the British Isles. In the eyes of the German High Command, victory was near. Hourly radio news bulletins brought the war into the living rooms of people across the Vineyard.

At the arraignment of Huntingdon Rice on August 6, the increased summer temperatures aggravated tensions that were already escalating between the district attorney and defense lawyer. Mr. Crossley's arrival in court was delayed that morning due to the capture of a suspect in another murder case, this one on the Cape. Court had to wait for his arrival on the next boat, and it was early afternoon before he arrived and the arraignment took place.

Crossley had requested that two experts testify on Huntingdon's mental health. They spent nearly three hours in an interview with Huntingdon in his cell. Their recommendations were not permitted in court, however, due to the strenuous objections of defense attorney Volpe, who contended their reports had not been made available to the defense, nor had they been properly filed in Edgartown. The defense attorney raised his voice as he stated that it was not usual to have the doctors report on "mentality" at an arraignment. He reminded the court to "hearken to the indictment!" The judge nodded at Volpe, who then accused Crossley of blatant collusion with the two physicians while they were aboard the ferry en route to the Vineyard that morning.

Crossley was irate. He stood up and responded loudly that he had only conversed with the two on the trip over. His intent was to expedite the trial, not jeopardize Mr. Rice. He denied his efforts were a grandstand play.

The judge refused to allow the experts to submit their report and limited the hearing to that of the arraignment. The *Gazette* reporter observed that Huntingdon did not exhibit any interest in the exchange, although he smiled as he chatted casually with his jailer, Nathan Mercer.

When Huntingdon was asked how he would plead to the charges, first in the case of rape and then murder, both times he answered, loudly and clearly, "not guilty."

Gossip in the courthouse hallways reported that the psychiatrists requested further observation of Huntingdon prior to filing their report.

Volpe admitted, "It's true that Mr. Rice is eccentric in some respects, but it does not follow he is a murderer."

In the Battle of Britain, the Nazi's Goering underestimated the number of Royal Air Force (RAF) planes. Although many planes had been shot down or destroyed on the ground, new planes and pilots had joined the force and the RAF deceived the Germans through camouflage and hiding of planes.

The Luftwaffe anticipated a victorious attack on August 18. However, the RAF was able to track German planes with radar and made direct hits. The Luftwaffe lost sixty-nine planes to thirty-one for the British.

In a speech before the House of Commons on August 20, Prime Minister Winston Churchill praised his fighter pilots. "Never in the field of human conflict was so much owed by so many to so few." "So few" became the nickname for the airmen of the Royal Air Force.

A week later the Luftwaffe bombed London.

Deep in the dog days of August, a *Gazette* reporter, perhaps Betty Hough herself, as she spent a lot of time in the courtroom, observed that Huntingdon was better dressed than the judge. Huntingdon looked quite natty in a new blue suit and his manner was remarkably calm. Judge Hanify, on the other hand, grew agitated because he had misplaced his robe. There was a delay in the proceedings until another robe could be located and once more there was order in the court.

This time the judge allowed the report by the psychiatrists to be submitted. Crossley and Volpe hunched over the table to peruse the handwritten pages. Judge Hanify agreed that Huntingdon should undergo further observation on his "mentality."

Huntingdon was thus committed to Bridgewater for thirty-five days of observation to determine his sanity. He would either be deemed sane, and stand trial for the rape and murder of Mrs. Smith, or considered insane, and institutionalized.

In other articles published in the *Gazette* as the Vineyard neared the end of the summer of 1940, Henry Hough editorialized on the names Fifteenth and Sixteenth Streets in the Ocean Heights section of Edgartown. He noted these appellations were chosen in 1903 when the area was considered ripe for development. To change the street names, he felt, was a decision that should be made by the residents who now lived there.

Also in road news, a favorite topic of the *Gazette*, it was reported the town of Vineyard Haven would pave an unfinished section of Franklin Street. State officials decreed only naturalized or native-born citizens would be permitted to work. No aliens, or immigrants, were allowed to participate on this project, budgeted to cost $9,000.

Red Sox left fielder Ted Williams pitched, that's right, pitched the final two innings of a game as the Sox lost to the league-leading Detroit Tigers. The Splendid Splinter surrendered three hits and a run, but struck out Tiger slugger Rudy York.

To retaliate against the bombing of civilian sites in London, Churchill ordered that the Royal Air Force bomb Berlin on August 24. Germans were dumbstruck that the RAF could attack, because it was assumed to be near collapse.

Irate at the British act of aggression, Hitler shifted his bombers away from British airfields and exclusively bombed urban areas. The East End of London was hit extremely hard. Brits huddled in the underground during air raids. The bombing blitz of London continued through most of September. Air raids destroyed buildings in London, Bristol, Liverpool and Manchester. Hitler planned the invasion of Britain, with the code name Operation Sealion.

British determination, inspired by Winston Churchill, held strong. The RAF was able to regroup once the Luftwaffe switched from bombing airfields to bombing cities. Morale was high. On both sides of the Atlantic, the hope was that if Britain could ward off the German attack, the United States would then be persuaded to enter the war and defeat Germany.

When the Luftwaffe swooped in over London on September 15, they were confronted by an onslaught of British planes, five full squadrons of Hurricanes and Spitfires. Fighting in the skies over London was extremely brutal. That afternoon the RAF raised twenty-eight squadrons against the Luftwaffe and decimated them, downing more than sixty German planes. This dogfight effectively ended Hitler's dream of destroying the British air force. There would be no invasion of Britain. The RAF Fighter Command had outlasted the German Luftwaffe and survived the Battle of Britain.

British success in holding off Hitler became a legend in America. Now it was hoped that the United States would soon join forces to defeat the Nazis.

The temperature on the Vineyard during mid-September ranged from a low of fifty-six to a high of eighty-four. It was a sultry time of year, with the air stagnant for long, dry spells. Vineyarders and vacationers made the most of the waning days of summer, while Huntingdon languished in Bridgewater.

chapter six

THE TRIAL OF RALPH HUNTINGDON RICE

News in late September included a report that the home of Betty Alden, daughter of John and Priscilla, built in 1669, was on the market. Stephen Luce Jr. became the first jockey to win the amateur trotting event cup at the Eastern States Exposition two years in a row. Luce was again astride Calumet Doble. A literary publication included an article, previously penned by Phidelah Rice, entitled, "The Art of Impersonation in Play Reading." It noted that Mr. Rice was the leading monactor in the country.

Helen Keller visited Katharine Cornell at her home, Chip-Chop, in Vineyard Haven. High school students greeted Miss Keller with a celebration of her sixtieth birthday. Miss Keller appreciated the Vineyard's wildflowers, as she was familiar with their scent and configuration, and she compared the Vineyard to the land of Peter Pan.

In a wide-ranging interview with the *Gazette,* Miss Keller spoke about Norse explorers, who were said to have visited the Vineyard. She had heard about the deaf community in Chilmark from her friend Alexander Graham Bell. Regarding the war, Miss Keller said, "That is true deaf-blindness on the part of the world." She was certain England would win the conflict with Germany.

Governor Leverett Saltonstall promulgated guidelines for a military draft. Town clerks across the Commonwealth were assigned registration responsibilities. Eligible males on the Vineyard and Nantucket, between the ages of twenty-one and thirty-six, were required to register in Falmouth on October 16. This was more than a year before the United States entered the war.

In a late September game, the Red Sox slammed six home runs against the Philadelphia Athletics. Slugger Jimmie Foxx hit his five hundredth homer, and Joe Cronin and Ted Williams also connected, yet the Sox slumped comfortably into fourth place.

Social news in the *Gazette* noted that William Everett Moll, actor, property man and assistant at the Rice Playhouse, traveled off island to play Friar Tuck in *Robin Hood*. He intended to return for the annual Vineyard Haven nativity play.

A bold advertisement promoted the new 1941 Ford, the biggest ever, built with semiconcealed running boards. The island movie theater in Oak Bluffs offered a double feature, Hopalong Cassidy in *Hidden Gold* and Lucille Ball in *You Can't Fool Your Wife*. Adults paid thirty cents for the matinee, juniors twenty cents and children a mere dime.

Henry Hough reviewed the just-ended summer season. He reflected on the bleak spring weather, the war and of course the murder of Clara Smith. The season did not get going until nearly August, Hough observed, then ended on Labor Day, while typically it ran from mid-June through mid-September. Next year he hoped would be better.

Balmy weather flooded the island, with temperatures ranging from the fifties into the high seventies during the last week of September, a pleasant time of year. Daylight savings time ended September 29.

Huntingdon was brought back from Bridgewater to the county jail in Edgartown after his stay in the state hospital. While the report from the psychiatrists was sealed, the implication was that he was competent to stand trial for the murder of Mrs. Smith. Headlines in the *Gazette* confirmed the rumors. "Rice, Found Sane, Is to be Tried Sept. 30."

Belmont Judge Raoul Henri Beaudreau was to preside over the superior court trial. It was his first assignment in Dukes County. The two-story, square, red brick courthouse, built in 1858, bustled with activity as it was readied for the trial. The sturdy structure was impressive, framed under a stand of oak and firmly stationed on Main Street, three blocks up from the harbor, adjacent to the popular old Whaling Church.

The Rice family assembled an aggressive team to defend Huntingdon. Besides Volpe, Alfred Walton of Boston was brought on, as well as Frank Vera, who split his time between the Vineyard and New Bedford. It was rumored the Christian Science Church financed the defense in an effort to clear the name of the church, as well as that of the defendant.

The Trial of Ralph Huntingdon Rice

Edgartown has been the county seat of Dukes County since 1642. This stately red brick courthouse is the most impressive brick building on the Vineyard. *Courtesy of Bob Aldrin.*

Volpe submitted a motion to request particulars of the crime, specifically when the murder occurred, the exact location, the weapon used and whether the offense was premeditated. He sought the names of the grand jurors who approved the indictment in July and the report from the medical examiner.

In addition, Volpe requested a copy of each day's testimony and submitted a list of a dozen witnesses. They included Pearl Blakeney, Carolee Rice, Elizabeth Rice, her eighty-seven-year-old mother Cora Pooler, Reverend Bernard Rice, Lydia Kipp, Lydia McClure, Marjorie Massow, Ruella Robertson, Milton Schwartz, Douglas John Kinser and William Everett Moll.

The defense also requested to see the actual letter Huntingdon mailed to his Christian Science confidante. Assistant District Attorney Frank Smith stood in for the campaigning district attorney. Smith argued that the defense should not be permitted to have a copy of the letter Huntingdon had sent to Edna White. He claimed the defense had no more right to a copy of the letter than if a plastic model of a bullet or a knife were allowed. Huntingdon's attorney, Walton, responded that since so much of the case hinged on the letter, it was only fair that a copy be provided to the defense.

Judge Beaudreau allowed the defense to view the letter under the watchful eye of state police Captain John Stokes, the same Captain Stokes who had overseen the initial investigation.

DEFENCE OPENS IN RICE TRIAL

Huntingdon Rice (center) strode assuredly into the courthouse. Superior Court Justice Robert Beaudreau donated a scrapbook of news clippings to the Martha's Vineyard Museum in 1970. The justice's father, Raoul, presided over the trial and collected the photos. *Courtesy of the Martha's Vineyard Museum.*

Jury selection began Monday morning, September 30. From a pool of sixty jurors, forty-seven were questioned. Dismissals or challenges ranged from overage to ill health to economic hardship. One juror was excused because of an allergy to ragweed and another was a master pilot on the ferries.

In the jurors' impaneling, a key question was their attitude on the death penalty. Vehement statements were uttered by prospective jurors on the issue, which, as Judge Beaudreau pointed out, was the penalty for first-degree murder. If found guilty, Huntingdon would "suffer the punishment of death in this State."

Nelson Hinckley said he would never agree to the electric chair and was excused. Arthur West voiced his opinion, "I don't believe in capital punishment," and was dismissed, as was Stuart Avery, who said, "I don't think I would send a man to the death sentence." One prospective juror could not grasp the concept of beyond a reasonable doubt. He said, "I can't get it right. Repeat it again," and was dismissed.

Clarence Allen of Gosnold was excused because he did not know whether he was related to the defendant. Walter Besse was told to remove his smoked glasses, so his face could be seen, and he was accepted. By three o'clock that afternoon, twelve jurors had been selected:

Walter Besse, Oak Bluffs, lineman
Howard Edwards, Oak Bluffs, fireman
Allen Flanders, Chilmark, retired
Walter Flanders, Tisbury, foreman
Hariph Hancock, Tisbury, contractor
Ernest Jenkinson, Chilmark, carpenter
George King, Gosnold, fisherman
Percival McDonough, Tisbury, merchant
Richard Morris, Oak Bluffs, meat cutter
George Tilton, Tisbury, painter
Charles Vanderhoop, Gay Head, retired light keeper
Benjamin West, Tisbury, clerk

No jurors were chosen from Edgartown; three came from Oak Bluffs. No alternate jurors were named. Soft-spoken, diffident Walter Flanders, a foreman at Hinckley's Lumber, was selected jury foreman.

Judge Beaudreau acknowledged that being away from families was a hardship, yet felt it imperative the jury be kept apart from outside influences or, as he phrased it, disturbances. "I haven't any doubt at all, but what

TUESDAY, OCTOBER 1, 1940

Defendant and Counsel at Edgartown Courthouse

Left to Right—Frank G. Volpe, Boston, defense counsel; Ralph Huntington Rice, charged with murder, and Alfred C. Walton, Boston, assistant to Volpe.

Defense Attorney Frank Volpe (left) consulted with assistant Alfred Walton (right) as defendant Huntingdon Rice looked on. *Courtesy of the Martha's Vineyard Museum.*

the case has been discussed more or less here on this Island," he said. He admonished his charges, "I do not want you to be distracted by any outside conversation at all." Then he sequestered them.

The trial got off to a rousing start. Assistant District Attorney Frank Smith stated that Huntingdon had already admitted his guilt. Volpe retorted, "I don't believe you intended to say that." To which Smith responded, "I do mean it! Rice told Captain Stokes, 'I know I am guilty.'"

During this interchange, Rice fumbled with his glasses, which appeared thick and awkward. He did not react to the flare-up between the attorneys. After that dramatic opening, the trial quickly settled down.

Judge Beaudreau explained to the jurors that attorneys would identify items and sites they believed were germane to the case. Comments would be designed to help the jurors comprehend testimony. On their tour of the crime scene, the judge sent officers to provide security and then added a final admonition to the jurors: "I assume that all of you have got raincoats or overcoats with you." The weather had turned stormy.

Judge Beaudreau (left) oversaw the trial of Huntingdon Rice (right), who was charged in the murder of Clara Smith. *Courtesy of the Martha's Vineyard Museum.*

The scene on East Chop was desolate when the jurors toured the school campus. Summer residents were long gone, lawns were untended, trash blew about and rain poured down, lashed by a chilly northeast breeze. "Gloomy indeed," moaned the *Gazette*. Fedoras, topcoats and slickers, with collars turned up against the wind, were the order of the day.

The jury was directed through Sumner Hall. They traipsed into the Rice house, around the playhouse and observed the park bench by the post office on Circuit Avenue where Huntingdon allegedly added a postscript in his letter to Edna White. The prosecutor pointed out that the Rice house was about two hundred paces from Sumner Hall.

Back in court, the charges against Rice were recited in blunt terms: "The murder was committed with deliberately premeditated malice aforethought, with extreme atrocity and cruelty, in the commission of the crime of rape or in an attempt to commit rape." Rice was charged with murder, committed between midnight and 2:30 a.m. in room fifteen of Sumner Hall.[11]

Rice Trial Jury at Scene of Murder

MEMBERS SHOWN OUTSIDE SUMNER HALL, OAK BLUFFS DORMITORY IN WHICH CRIME WAS COMMITTED.

Members of the jury huddled in the rain by Sumner Hall during an on-site visit to the scene of the crime. *Courtesy of the Martha's Vineyard Museum.*

The Commonwealth presented opening arguments on the injuries sustained and the cause of death. No murder weapon was ever described or located. On the charge of rape, the Commonwealth could not state whether it had occurred when Mrs. Smith was unconscious or even dead.

Recounting the scene of the crime, Assistant District Attorney Smith noted that the room was in "shambles." Photographs showed the extent of Clara's injuries, "bearing out the state's contention that the crime was committed with great atrocity and extreme cruelty."

According to the prosecutor, Rice claimed he knew nothing of the murder until Monday afternoon, July 1. However, about 10:15 on Sunday morning, the day before his alleged knowledge, Rice had been seen at Keating's Drugstore on Circuit Avenue, where he bought stamps and mailed a letter to New York. It was postmarked Sunday, June 30, at 11:00 a.m., less than three hours after the body of Mrs. Smith was discovered.

Smith addressed the jurors.

> *The letter in a general way states that a woman had been murdered, that the body had been found and that the police had taken charge of the situation. Rice claimed he knew nothing of the murder when the letter was dispatched, but the state will show you that it must have been mailed even before 11 am, because of the regulation which fixes the time for changing the date on the cancellation stamps in the post offices.*

Thus, Smith showed his hand in an effort to prove Rice's guilt, essentially through the incriminating letter.

The first witness was an engineer, Clifford Dugan, who described the layout of Sumner Hall and how it was connected to the Club House. A staircase led to the second and third floors of the dormitory.

Court broke for lunch. When it reconvened, the Tuesday afternoon session played out like a tour of a photographer's studio. Commercial photographer Augustus Merry introduced photos from the crime scene, taken between 11:15 a.m. and 12:15 p.m. on June 30. The shots revealed blood spattered on the wall, a blanket drawn over Mrs. Smith's face, a small table with Christian Science books, an open window, clothing strewn about and the tipped-over wastebasket.

Huntingdon did not look at the photographs; he either glanced down at the floor or fixed his eyes on a window in the courtroom. He indicated no interest in what was going on around him.

Walter Tomkins, a state police photographer, also took shots of the crime scene. Two additional photographs were introduced that had been taken at the Martha's Vineyard Funeral Home.

Clarence Lester Smith, stepson of the deceased, testified he last saw his mother on June 6. When he and his wife arrived on the Vineyard, the day after his mother's death, they visited Mrs. Phidelah Rice and May Rice.

The prosecutor called Dr. Buckley, who was a graduate of Boston University Medical School. He testified that the death occurred six hours prior to his arrival at the crime scene, at about 2:30 a.m. At the crime scene, Dr. Buckley had found a small leather purse that contained fifteen dollars.

The *Vineyard Gazette* summarized the autopsy: "The report was long and technical, but its scientific language did not conceal the gruesome and sordid

MRS. PEARL H. BLAKNEY

orchester woman, who told of dis
overing slain woman's body wher
he testified yesterday at the Edgar
town trial.

Pearl Blakeney, traveling companion of the victim, met Clara Smith through the Christian Science church in Dorchester. *Courtesy of the Martha's Vineyard Museum.*

nature of the findings recorded." Human hair had to be pried from Mrs. Smith's clenched fist. Clearly the death was neither an accident nor suicide, Dr. Buckley said, in response to a question. The weapon must have had a sharp edge or a flat side, and probably more than two blows were struck. Mrs. Smith had been strangled. Her ring finger was terribly injured, most likely when the ring was wrenched off.

Dr. Alan Moritz, an assistant in pathology at the state department of public safety, testified that death came approximately six to ten hours after she had dinner, and she died within minutes of the severe blows to her head.

The next witness was Mrs. Smith's companion, Pearl Ella Blakeney. With a bright, attractive face and a brisk step, she arrived in court wearing a blue dress buttoned down the front, with a smart white collar. Her blue hat was adorned with a tiny red ribbon, and she hid her face behind a blue veil. The *Gazette* reported, "She spoke distinctly, and there was an intimation that her courses in diction at the Rice School, where she was instructed for three successive terms by the defendant, Ralph Huntingdon Rice, had something to do with her clear, pleasant pronunciation."

Crossley had advised her not to return to the island until the trial, so she would not be influenced by talk on the street. Blakeney stated she had been employed as a file clerk for Western Union for the past fifteen years. She testified that Huntingdon had always behaved like a gentleman in her presence, and that she studied diction with him, as well as a course in Bible reading. Blakeney shyly admitted she came from Canada and explained she attended the Rice School because "I had a very poor vowel sound." Judge Beaudreau warned against laughter.

Blakeney testified that Mrs. Smith suffered from shortness of breath after walking, but had no other medical ailments that she was aware of. The night before the murder, Blakeney had seen a man go upstairs at Sumner Hall, look at the ceiling beneath room fifteen, come down and then walk across the verandah and down to the beach. It was about 6:00 p.m. She did not recognize the man, nor did she ever see him again. The identity of this mystery man was never revealed.

She recounted the night of the murder. At first, she said, it seemed like a nightmare, then "like someone trying to talk who couldn't." She heard some thumps, "as if someone might have taken a shoe and hit on the wall or floor with the heel." She recounted that there were three or four thumps.

"We had always gone down to breakfast together," she said of the subsequent morning. "Whichever was ready first called for the other. I knocked at Mrs. Smith's door, and there was no response. I knocked three times."

She described how horrified she was when she found the victim. "I saw a face I thought was a corpse."

Blakeney said it was possible Mrs. Smith had misplaced her ring, as she was wont to do, once leaving it in a washstand and another time on a train.

The next witness was Lydia Jane Kipp from Columbus, Ohio. Both Kipp and Huntingdon had stayed at the Rice house in June when she was acting as the school's secretary. She reported Huntingdon often complained about his inability to sleep, and added she once heard him up and about at 4:00 a.m., on the telephone.

The "fearful look" Huntingdon cast at her that Saturday night after the murder was considered a link to the crime. Volpe contended the police thought Huntingdon was guilty because he was crazy, and the fearful look at Kipp just added to their suspicion.

Kipp moved into room thirteen at Sumner Hall—the room across the hall from Pearl Blakeney—on June 28. During her testimony, it was brought out that Huntingdon had stayed at the Club House four years ago; hence, he was familiar with the layout of the dormitory.

In Volpe's cross-examination, Kipp revealed that Tracy arrived May 30. She testified that he worked as an electrician and drove the beach wagon that picked up Mrs. Smith. And it was Tracy who took her bags up to her room. This was the foundation in the groundwork of Volpe's strategy, which was to link Harold Tracy to the crime.

Kipp explained that Tracy was involved in an affair with Marjorie Massow, a young student at the school. She reported that the women in the Bible reading class, of whom Mrs. Smith had been a spokesperson, were appalled that Tracy chased after young Marjorie. They wanted the relationship to end. That, of course, infuriated Tracy. "He [Tracy] made the threat that he was going to get even with these Bible women," testified Kipp.

Now Kipp found herself in the middle of the trial, with testimony that implicated both Harold Tracy and Ralph Huntingdon Rice. Both sides listened carefully to her every word.

As school secretary, it was Kipp's responsibility to collect payments for tuition and board. That fateful night she held Mrs. Smith's check, as well as over $1,000 in payments from other students, as she slept three rooms away from the crime scene. Had the intruder known the money was in room thirteen, Kipp would likely have been the victim.

On cross-examination, Volpe asked Kipp her opinion of Huntingdon. "You thought that he was pampered and petted by his family, spoiled by them, is that right?" "Yes," said Kipp. "And that his family avoided telling him any unpleasant things?" "Yes," said Kipp.

Huntingdon had never made inappropriate advances toward her, nor anyone else that she knew of. "They kicked about his being a tough teacher," she said. Volpe asked, "They thought he was queer, didn't they?"

MISS LYDIA JANE KIPP

It was the wide-eyed glance Huntingdon shot school secretary Lydia Kipp that landed him on the hot seat with the state police. *Courtesy of the Martha's Vineyard Museum.*

And she did too? Miss Kipp said yes to both questions, but reiterated that Huntingdon was always a gentleman.

Volpe recounted a confrontation between Huntingdon and Kipp. "A foolish argument," said Kipp.

Volpe retold the tale. "You came into the room and someone picked a coat off a chair, and you said you were glad that one person at least had manners. And Mr. Rice thought you shouldn't have talked that way to a teacher before students." "Yes," said Kipp. "He thought that you ought to apologize?" "Yes," said Kipp. "But you didn't?" "No I didn't," said Kipp.

Kipp saw no change in Huntingdon after the murder. He was always studious. She knew he was sickly and took little things seriously. He had to nap after lunch and became irritable when he didn't get his rest.

Martha Stingel of Melrose was another student in the school that summer. She was "a petite young woman in a white lace overblouse and a dark skirt," the *Gazette* reported. "She wore a small dark hat on the back of her head, revealing blonde curls at the front, and she wore sparkling earrings. She was alert and at ease on the stand."

Stingel testified to being awoken by someone muttering unintelligibly on the night of the murder. She recalled, "The noises I heard were as of someone having a nightmare. There were groans and mumbling as if someone was talking rather indistinctly and just a pounding as though someone was pounding on the mattress while they were having a dream, or something to that effect. It was not very sharp; it was just like a dull thud, pounding on the pillow or mattress."

One wonders why none of the students in the dormitory got up to see if they could comfort the person having such a bad dream.

Stenographer Elwin Hauver recorded the interrogation at state police headquarters on July 7. According to Hauver's notes, which he referred to frequently in his testimony, Huntingdon claimed he first heard of the murder when his sister May said she had to tell him something that would disturb him. He didn't want to hear, but she insisted. She said Mrs. Smith died of a heart attack, but the police said murder.

At Keatings, the soda jerk told Huntingdon he heard there had been an accident at the school. Huntingdon assumed that referred to Phidelah's arrival as an invalid. Huntingdon bought three three-cent stamps and a one-cent stamp and sent a special delivery letter to Edna White.

Huntingdon felt the police were after him early on. He explained he got nervous easily. He said he feared he would say something that would be held against him, and he did.

The night of the murder, he visited his brother Phidelah until 9:30 p.m., went upstairs to his room and was in bed by 10:30 p.m. At 5:00 a.m. he awoke to birds chirping outside and went down to breakfast. Later, he went to church with his sister-in-law and ate dinner, followed by his nap.

Huntingdon had observed Tracy in the company of a "nice young thing." He said that Tracy was often drunk and characterized him as "a clever city man" and a "pretty slick ticker."

Contents of the letter to Edna White were introduced. It detailed Huntingdon's nervous symptoms following a bad dream. He expressed relief that he was excused from the morning assembly for new students. It was only "through the kindness of my sister-in-law, who used to be so unkind, I was permitted to go back to bed and miss classes."

The incriminating postscript was read by Hauver. "One of the Bible students, a practitioner from Boston was found dead in her room yesterday morning. She was an old lady, about 75, and had a claim to heart disease. This has cast a pall over the student body and indicates evidence of malpractice. If ever there was an evil place, this is it."

According to Hauver's notes, Huntingdon was confronted by this letter, with the postscript, which police claimed demonstrated intimate prior knowledge of the murder. By the postmark on the envelope, the letter contradicted Huntingdon's claim that he did not know about the murder until the next day.

Hauver described the moment:

> *Mr. Rice looked at the letter closely. He looked at the envelope. There was a long pause in which no one spoke. There were sighs. He examined the postmark with a pocket microscope, looked around the room, up at the ceiling, and closed his eyes. Then he, well, I might say, grimaced. I saw perspiration start out on his forehead and trickle down. I noticed that his cheek was becoming flushed. This pause continued, for, I should say, as much as ten minutes.*

Smith interrupted to ask, "Then what happened?"

Hauver read Huntingdon's exact words. "Well, I know I am guilty...I am innocent, sir...I never knew about it until my sister told me. I must have used the wrong date."

During the interrogation, Hauver recorded twenty-four times that Captain Stokes asked Huntingdon about the letter, the postmark or the murder.

In his cross-examination, Volpe questioned Hauver as to where the letter and envelope had been found. Hauver said Inspector Michael Murphy indicated they came from two different places in Edna White's New York apartment. The letter was in a book and the envelope was tucked in the drawer of a nearby desk. Nothing proved that letter belonged in that envelope.

The prosecutor called Captain Stokes to the stand. He stated he took Huntingdon into custody at 1:10 p.m. Sunday afternoon, July 7. Huntingdon claimed he had not eaten since breakfast and was offered a sandwich and buttermilk. May and Elizabeth Rice tried to visit him, but because he was in police custody during the interrogation, they were not permitted to converse with him. They sat in their car by the police barracks at Dr. Tucker's house.

Stokes admitted he had talked about Huntingdon's mental condition and considered him crazy. Judge Beaudreau asked if Rice was under arrest when he was on the porch. Stokes said he was not. "But you didn't tell him that he need not answer your questions, did you?" the judge asked. Smith interrupted, "That isn't the law." (The Miranda decision, which gave suspects the right to remain silent to avoid self-incrimination, was handed down in 1966, twenty-six years later.)

Chief Amaral described the victim's room. No one considered that the night table could have been the murder weapon.

The prosecution rested the Commonwealth's case at 3:15 p.m. on Friday, October 4. Seventeen of thirty witnesses had testified.

Volpe presented opening remarks for the defense the next day, Saturday morning. He vowed there would be no claim of insanity as a defense. Nor would he call any high-priced experts to the stand, he promised, in a sharp rebuke to the district attorney.

When Huntingdon was first questioned by the police on July 3, he stated he was a member of the faculty and implied he was too busy to consult with the police because he had to keep an appointment. Once he was persuaded to submit to questioning, he revealed that his appointment was to take a nap.

Volpe laid out his case. The Bible women, a group that had included Mrs. Smith, "will so testify that Tracy was going to get even because they stopped him going around with this girl." The case was not about Huntingdon, Volpe stated; rather, Harold Tracy should be on trial.

The defense called its first witness. New York police inspector Michael Murphy spoke with a brogue as he recounted that he went to 41 Central Park West to see Mrs. White. Huntingdon had been writing her almost daily in June.

Murphy asked if she had any letters from Huntingdon. When she furnished a letter, he asked for the envelope. She rummaged in a desk drawer and pulled out an old one. The inspector noticed the dates didn't match. She said it was probably an envelope from a different letter. This was not conveyed to Stokes or Crossley.

The defense called Lewis Dow, assistant Oak Bluffs postmaster for the past thirty years. He was described by the *Gazette* as "gentle, soft-spoken and white haired." Dow stated that postal regulations clearly forbid him from testifying in court. He said, "I call your attention to Section 702, paragraph 9, of the postal regulations." The judge said he was required to testify. This was a murder trial and his testimony was imperative to prove the guilt or innocence of the defendant.

Dow acquiesced and proceeded to explain that date stamps were changed to 11:00 a.m. the night before mail was sent off island. At 11:10 a.m. on June 30, the stamp was changed to 4:00 p.m., and later to 5:00 a.m. July 1. The mail closed at 11:10 on the morning of June 30, which was the first day for summer mail service.

Huntingdon's incriminating letter left the Vineyard in the South Postal Annex pouch on the afternoon boat, and made its way to Boston by 8:30 p.m. It arrived in New York City early the next morning and was delivered to Edna White.[12]

Volpe developed his strategy to set the stage to prove Huntingdon's innocence. He said, "We are going to show that this man had this deceased in his class, she was one of the Bible class of five, and a fine lady, a gentle lady."

Volpe then described the Rice household. He noted Phidelah Rice slept on a couch in the dining room, his wife tending to him every half hour through the night. Mrs. Rice's mother, Elizabeth Pooler, slept in the adjacent sun porch. May, Huntingdon and Carolee Rice had rooms upstairs. The implication was that for Huntingdon to leave and return, five people would have been aware of his movements. No one heard Huntingdon go outside that night.

Carolee Rice had been to a dance at the Tivoli with her girlfriends. She went upstairs about 12:30 a.m., but couldn't fall asleep until nearly 2:00. Her door was open to let in a breeze. She heard her uncle cough several times.

At 5:00 a.m. Huntingdon was seen by Mrs. Pooler in the kitchen, in his nightshirt and dressing gown, preparing breakfast. He went back to bed and wrote a letter to Mrs. White, complaining about his nervous condition. At 10:00 a.m. he went downtown to Keatings for stamps to mail his letter.

Huntingdon sang in church that Sunday morning after the murder. Volpe asked sarcastically if that was evidence of guilt. He sought an analysis of the hair found in Mrs. Smith's hand, and of the fingerprints and bloodstains at the scene of the crime. None of his requests were honored.

Volpe revisited the interrogation at state police headquarters. He claimed the officers harassed Huntingdon, saying he was going to the electric chair and challenging his Christian Science beliefs. "They had the best detectives in the state there—in the world—and after fourteen hours he still told the same story," said Volpe.

Harold Tracy had his eye on Marjorie Massow, Volpe contended. Tracy was drunk when he left Stag Cottage at 1:40 a.m. in the beach wagon. He wrote a letter to Massow in which he stated the police would try to pin the murder on him. If they did, he threatened to commit suicide. When he was confronted with the letter during interrogation by the police, he was arrested on the concealed weapon charge.

Volpe called May Rice, Huntingdon's sister, to the stand. She had served as general supervisor of the school since 1932, and had been affiliated with it since its inception.

Volpe asked about Huntingdon's capacity to return to teach this summer. She testified, "He has been very nervous, increasingly so, and it has been very difficult for him to carry on his work here at the school in the summertime." Huntingdon returned, reluctantly, because he was needed. He looked and acted quite ill during June, she testified, sleeping poorly with constant trips to the bathroom.

"It was a family custom to keep unpleasant news from him," she said. The Rice house was "of summer construction," which made it very easy to hear what transpired in nearby rooms. A sign on Huntingdon's door often read, "resting, please do not disturb."

On Sunday, June 30, May Rice awoke at 6:00 a.m. and went to the Club House to oversee breakfast service. Pearl Blakeney rushed downstairs to her shortly after 8:00 a.m. "Something terrible has happened. I think Mrs. Smith is dead. There is blood everywhere."

Rice said, "I objected to calling the police because I didn't want to excite the girls." Hence, when they were called, the police arrived in plain clothes and were not posted on the premises until later that afternoon. Rice conferred with her sister-in-law Elizabeth and decided to withhold news of the murder from Phidelah, Huntingdon and Elizabeth's mother, Mrs. Pooler.

Rice herself telephoned Edna White on Monday evening because Huntingdon acted unusually nervous that afternoon, after she had disclosed the murder to him. She was present when the police took Huntingdon in for questioning on Sunday, July 7. She and Carolee drove to the police barracks, but were not allowed in. The women sat in their car and waited. May Rice remained outside the barracks until three in the morning, when her brother was formally charged with murder.

Mrs. Phidelah (Elizabeth) Rice took the stand and, according to the *Gazette* report, spoke with her "clear, well modulated voice [which] testified to her long training in voice culture." She assumed the role of the grand dame. In her testimony, she affirmed Huntingdon was "singing lustily" when he was in church that Sunday morning after the murder.

Of Huntingdon's behavior, his sister-in-law testified, "He was so extremely nervous, everything affected him so quickly that we learned to be very, very careful in handling him."

She was justified in excusing Huntingdon from the opening assembly, but expected him to teach his new classes, which began Tuesday. He was not aware his niece Carolee had enrolled in his class. Unknown issues could set him off. She stated Huntingdon was conscientious, but "his condition made it difficult to live with him." When he did not have his nap, he could be quite disagreeable, she said.

Carolee was the third Rice woman who took the stand that day. She had attended high school in Vineyard Haven and considered herself almost a native. After church on June 30, she drove down to meet the 11:40 boat to pick up students for the second term. It was when she dropped the students off at Sumner Hall that she learned of the murder.

Testimony concluded on Saturday, October 5, and was continued to Monday, October 7.

A little banter occurred between the attorneys: "I think I'll withdraw my objection and let it go without objection," said Smith with a smile. "It took you a long time to make up your mind," said Volpe. "I have a reason," said Smith. "We don't care about your reason," said Volpe.

Lydia Rich McClure, dietitian and housemother, ran the kitchen, ordered the food, paid the bills and ensured rooms were ready for incoming students. McClure went to bed at 11:30 p.m. on Saturday, June 29. Her room was on the street level of Sumner Hall and the doors around her were closed, but not locked. All the doors in the three-story dormitory were unlocked.

The next morning when McClure began to prepare breakfast for Mrs. Smith, May Rice said she did not think Mrs. Smith would need any breakfast that morning. "I was told she had a shock of some kind," said McClure.

When she visited room fifteen, McClure testified, "I noticed that the covers were thrown back, the center of the pillow being filled with blood." Under cross-examination she acknowledged Huntingdon had asked her details about the murder after he was told about it Monday afternoon.

Edna White, of 41 Central Park West, New York City, was called. "A slender, attractive woman in a yellow hat and veil, a brown figured dress, and a fur cape over her shoulders," noted the *Gazette*. "She wore white gloves. Her face was alert, and her eyes particularly animated."

She had been Huntingdon's practitioner since 1932, treating him for "nervous trouble, insomnia and throat trouble." She expounded on her religious beliefs. "A Christian Scientist realizes the truth about God and His care. Man is made in the image and likeness of God, and God is the foundation of the Bible. It is based upon the King James version of the Bible and upon the text book, *Science and Health with Key to the Scriptures* by Mary Baker Eddy."[13]

MRS. ELIZABETH P. RICE   MISS MAE B. RICE

Elizabeth Rice cared for her invalid husband all summer; May Rice tried to protect her students from news of the murder. *Courtesy of the Martha's Vineyard Museum.*

As a practitioner, White said her role was to explain the truths of spiritual understanding that Huntingdon already understood. She wrote him to verify these truths, which allowed him the opportunity to share his emotional and physical well-being with her.

She admitted there was a good deal of correspondence in late June 1940. Huntingdon sent White a dollar for airmail stamps to make their correspondence even more rapid. Besides frequent letters and phone calls, he also telegraphed her at least three times.

Volpe asked whether her treatments succeeded. Smith challenged him. Volpe rebutted, "The supreme court has said a Christian Science practitioner is the same as a doctor." The challenge was denied. White stated that she measured the success of her treatment by the tone and substance of what Huntingdon wrote in his letters. She answered them as quickly as possible.

Christian Scientist doctrine mandates that correspondence between practitioners and patients be confidential. White pointed to the page in the manual regarding confidentiality. Another regulation stated letters were to be destroyed as soon as answered.

Regarding the visit by Inspector Murphy, White initially determined to keep the correspondence confidential. When Murphy threatened her with complicity in the crime if she failed to cooperate, she produced the letter with the incriminating postscript. When she gave him the letter, he had trouble reading it. "This here, this man, he has a peculiar, a queer handwriting," Murphy said to her.

After a few minutes, Murphy asked her for the envelope to the letter. White stated she looked around for it, and then "I opened the middle drawer of my desk, rummaged around, and underneath papers, I found this one envelope without a letter in it."

Under cross-examination by Smith, White stuck by her story that the letter and envelope were not together. Smith did not question why she failed to destroy the letter, as mandated by the Christian Science manual.

Volpe introduced another letter, this one from May Rice to White, written shortly after his arrest. "I know you are standing by in this terrible thing which has come to us. Your wire came this morning and I handed it to my brother through the bars. That seems too awful to write. I am afraid he cannot stand the strain. There is no evidence except that he acted so nervous, too nervous for an innocent man, they said."

In a subsequent letter to White, May Rice observed it appeared the letter of July 1 was inadvertently put with the envelope postmarked June 30. That would account for the discrepancy in dates. "He was writing to you almost every day and it would have been the easiest thing in the world to put a letter in an envelope of another date." Of course, that is exactly what happened.

Edna White was superintendent of the Second Church of Christ Sunday school in New York City. During the trial she was taunted for staying at the posh Charlotte Inn. *Courtesy of the Martha's Vineyard Museum.*

The attorneys haggled over the letters: "You destroyed some?" asked Smith. "She said she destroyed one," said Volpe. "Can't you understand English?" "As well as you do," said Smith.

A moment later, "Do you want to come up here and help me?" asked Smith when Volpe mumbled something inaudible. "I don't want to be near you," said Volpe. "Probably that's the safest way," said Smith.

"What letter are you talking about?" asked Volpe. "Do you want to try both sides of the case?" inquired Smith. "If I can't understand, she can't," said Volpe. "Why don't you listen?" asked Smith.

In another conflict in personalities, Judge Beaudreau addressed the attorneys. "In order to keep the record straight, I wish you would give me a chance to speak on these matters before going ahead. I haven't had that chance very much lately."

Volpe read into the record White's response to a letter written by Huntingdon. "I am giving you metaphysical treatments. I also know that you will prove, and in all confidence, your innocence. Mrs. Eddy [Mary Baker Eddy] says, 'truth is not lost in the midst of remoteness of the barbarisms of spiritless codes.'"

Court testimony covered more than sixty pages on the letters between White and Huntingdon. White testified she was aware Huntingdon had been indicted. "However," she added, "I was not aware that you were convicting a man on an envelope dug up from nowhere."[14]

Mrs. White answered the June 30 letter that indicated Rice was in good spirits and improving health. That was the letter Rice showed Crossley, which indicated Rice had correspondence off island and led to further interrogation, arrest and trial.

In his effort to introduce Harold Tracy into the trial once more, Volpe pursued three acquaintances who testified under oath to have seen Tracy Saturday night. Douglas John Kinser was a student; Milton Schwartz and William Everett Moll were employed by the playhouse. Schwartz and Moll said Tracy returned to Stag Cottage, located behind the theatre, at 1:00 a.m. from a night of heavy drinking downtown. Tracy drove off in the beach wagon between 1:30 and 1:45 a.m.

Moll testified that Tracy said, "I am going out tonight to get a woman, and I don't give a damn if she is an Indian."

Schwartz testified Tracy was drunk. Very drunk. "He drove away in the station wagon about quarter to two. Didn't see him again until next morning."

On Sunday, June 30, Tracy asked Schwartz to cover for him. "If the police should ask you about us, say I was with you all Saturday night." Schwartz responded, "Don't be silly. What can they do to you?" To which Tracy said, "Well, they pin these things on you."

Kinser testified that on the morning of June 30, "Tracy's condition was one of extreme nervousness. That he constantly referred to feeling sick in the stomach." Kinser went on. "Tracy said he had been on a hell of a bat the night before; he didn't know as he ever felt worse after a drunk."

Volpe's strategy was to pin a consciousness of guilt on Tracy, but the judge refused to allow any other questions. He said they were not germane to the case against Huntingdon.

Marjorie Massow was called to the stand. "Miss Massow, a striking looking brunette with a long bob of heavy brown hair, was smartly dressed," the *Gazette* gushed. Henry Hough described her as "eighteen, so dark and so pretty—and as the attorneys emphasize—so innocent." She had been Rice's pupil and had nothing derogatory to say about him. He had taught her in both group and private sessions.

"Did Thomas [Harold Tracy] ever say to you that he would get even with the Bible women?" Volpe asked, but the question was excluded by the judge because it was not about Huntingdon.

Massow had gone out with Tracy that summer. She had a special nickname for him, but he had told her not to repeat it in court. She knew about his past, but again, she testified that Tracy did not want her to divulge it. These tantalizing tidbits went unchallenged.

Massow's room was on the third floor of Sumner Hall, directly above Mrs. Smith's. When she and her roommate Ruella Robertson returned from the movies that Saturday night, she noticed the outside doors were open, so she closed them.

Usually Massow drove the Bible women to church on Sunday mornings. When Mrs. Smith did not appear ready for church that morning, Massow started upstairs to get her. May Rice interceded and said she thought Mrs. Smith did not want to go to church that morning.

Reverend Bernard Rice took the stand to aver that Huntingdon had been ill since childhood and had often been cared for by their sister May. "We have all tried to shield him," said the Reverend.

The highlight of the trial that Monday morning was a surprise witness for the defense. Harold Thomas Tracy, aka Jan Thomas, took the stand. The *Gazette* noted every detail. "Tracy was neatly dressed, in a new-appearing, well-pressed blue suit, with pinstripes of white. He was clean shaven, except for a slender dark mustache, and his hair was of rather more than ordinary

GIRL STUDENTS TESTIFY

Assistant Defense Attorney Alfred Walton walked Marjorie Massow (left) and her roommate Ruella Robertson into court. The girls were students of Huntingdon Rice, who taught the speaking voice, which consisted of correct breathing, vocal support, breath control and elevation of the tongue. *Courtesy of the Martha's Vineyard Museum.*

length, well-barbered and combed carefully. He was pale, and seemed somewhat nervous."

Judge Beaudreau asked Tracy if he had consulted with counsel, and he had not. The judge warned, "It is my responsibility to inform you that you do not have to testify here if you do not wish to, and your failure to testify, if you do not, cannot be used against you."

"Tracy's countenance brightened visibly as the judge spoke," the *Gazette* reported, "and his voice, when he replied, was pleasant, as compared with the previous tones he had used."

Harold Tracy, dapper and dignified, testified for the defense. *Courtesy of the Martha's Vineyard Museum.*

"Yes," said Tracy, "I have nothing to hide. I don't mind testifying."

Because he was brought into court in defense of Huntingdon, Tracy was granted immunity from prosecution.

Tracy denied he met Mrs. Smith at the boat, or had carried her bags to her room. He claimed he only knew her by sight. He went downtown Saturday night, June 29, with Moll and Schwartz for a few drinks and then returned home. Tracy admitted, "I drove the beach wagon from where it had been parked on one side of the road near the cottage, around the tennis court, up into the yard."

Tracy referred to the letter he wrote Marjorie Massow, which went on for four pages. It concluded with the plaintive remark, "I'm tired of trying to find the happiness that is always just out of reach." He admitted he threatened suicide if the police suspected him of the murder.

The jailer's wife, Hattie Mercer, took the stand. When Tracy was incarcerated in the Edgartown jail, Mercer, testified, "He [Tracy] asked if he could send a letter right out if he wrote it; he wanted to find out who he was with and where he was that night."

Volpe asked, "Did he say to you, Mrs. Mercer, 'When I came out of a stupor that night, I found myself in a stairway in Sumner Hall?'"

Mercer stated, "He did. That is all he remembered of that night."

On cross-examination, Smith said, "You never told anybody the story that you have told here about Tracy being on the Sumner Hall steps of the dormitory, did you Madam."

"No sir," said Mercer.

Tracy was brought back on the stand. Under oath, he claimed he had never been in Sumner Hall that evening. Volpe asked, "And do you mean to say you didn't tell Mrs. Mercer that when you came out of your drunk you found yourself on the stairway of Sumner Hall?" Tracy recanted the entire story he had told Mrs. Mercer that summer.

Judge Beaudreau would not let him say anything else. "He has denied what Mrs. Mercer said, and that's all I'm going to permit," said the judge.

Henry Hough summed up the situation. "So ironically, the government seeks to establish an alibi for the man who was once its own alternate as he is the main defendant of [Rice's] counsel now."

Ralph Huntingdon Rice took the stand in his own defense at 12:30 p.m. on Tuesday, October 8. The *Boston Globe* reported, "Today the defendant, six feet tall, with the well-developed jaw of a singer, mild blue eyes and close-cropped brown hair," spoke for two hours on the stand. "He was calm, even under cross-examination, his voice ringing out crisp and clear."

The *Gazette* echoed with, "He seemed calm and self possessed. In a baritone voice, he spoke with the deliberation and clear cut accent that reveal the trained speaker. He smiled faintly at times, not in amusement, but in an apparent effort to be friendly and cooperative, and his hands, clasped over the rail of the dock, held with a firm but not tensed grip as he stood." Only his eyes, which roved around the room, belied his nervousness.

Huntingdon testified that on the night in question, he retired to his room in the family home on Arlington Street, where he sang for half an hour, read Christian Science literature and then went to bed. On his door he hung a sign that said he was resting and he was not to be disturbed.

He was excused from the Monday assembly. Instead, he spent his time deciding which lectures to give that week and reviewed the names of his new students in preparation for his Tuesday class. He taught each class assigned to him during that first week of July.

The police spoke with him on Wednesday. He relinquished his afternoon nap to speak with them, and that interview lasted three hours. Huntingdon said he was treated politely; so politely he shared with Crossley a letter he had recently received from his practitioner. It was, of course, that letter that led to his arrest.

The murder had affected him, causing the recent spate of nervousness. If one did not protect oneself from the traumas of the outside world, he said, one might fall under the clutches of the "mental atmosphere" of the murder.

On occasion, he ran for exercise. Huntingdon acknowledged he may have appeared out of breath when he reported the vandalized sign to Mr. Cook, and gave Miss Kipp the "fearful look."

Huntingdon testified about the interrogation at state police headquarters. He said, "If anyone could connect me with this crime in any way, it would be through perjury." He said there were two people who did not like him: Levy, a carpenter, and Harold Tracy (Thomas), the electrician. Tracy didn't like him because Huntingdon had warned Tracy not to hang around with Marjorie Massow or he would tell the housemother (McClure). Huntingdon didn't like the man's looks and knew he was a drunk. Despite Captain Stokes's badgering, Huntingdon said he could stay there ten hours but would never tell him more than what he had already said.

On the discrepancy over the misdated letter, Huntingdon said, "It's too much for me." He claimed a distinct memory for both the June 30 letter (buying stamps at Keatings) and the July 1 letter (the postscript about the murder). "I was hammered for I don't know how many hours."

He recounted a series of unprofessional taunts leveled at him by the officers. "Well, Rice, you're a pretty clever guy, you almost had us fooled," one officer jeered. Another said, "The perfect crime—almost. They always forget something." A third policeman said, "You ought to have waited till Monday to mail that letter. You might get away with that up in Chilmark, but not in this town."

Huntingdon explained that Officer Bradford said, "Now Rice, tell us where the loot is. Where's the instrument you murdered her with?" Another officer said, "They tell me you're a Christian Scientist. You're a fine Christian Scientist. You're going to the electric chair." Another said, "Look how badly he's perspiring. See how his hand is shaking! Innocent, hell, he sure looks guilty." Huntingdon said, "I told them they would be in the same state if they had had to go through all that strain."

When the prosecutor interjected a comment, the attorneys clashed once more: "Are you going to run this cross-examination or am I?" asked Smith. "Well, I'm behind you," replied Volpe. "So long as you stay behind," retorted Smith.

The prosecutor introduced "evidence he [Rice] was a man who suffered from some nervous disorder; that it so affected him that customarily he could not sleep nights." The defense rebutted that although Rice was a man of a nervous temperament, that did not make him a murderer.

Huntingdon admitted to insomnia, mostly in the summer. He said at times he would write a letter, but not mail it until he rewrote it. In an unmailed June 29 letter, he described complaints about the women he worked with, but then decided not to send such a letter to Mrs. White, as she was a woman. He had a high regard for women, but confessed to difficulty getting along with them. "Down here [Rice School] it is all women, teachers and co-workers."

He acknowledged that sometimes people thought that he appeared to be in a daze. Huntingdon claimed he always had a specific destination, whether to go to the bathroom, to his sister's room or to telephone Mrs. White.

He expressed relief at how he had weathered the incarceration. "I want to say that during the process of this dreadful suffering I have had to rise above many weaknesses. I have actually gained weight and strength and intellectual capacity." He gained fifteen pounds while in jail.

Testimony began again on October 9.

Mrs. Mercer introduced a letter Huntingdon wrote in jail, which she had turned over to the police on July 13. "You can't read that," said Volpe. "I'm looking at it," said Smith. "Go ahead and look at it and keep your mouth shut," said Volpe. "I will warn you men for the last time," said the judge. "You have got to be patient with one another until the end." No details of the letter were introduced in court.

The prosecution called Theodore Levy. The prosecution asked, "Where do you live?" Levy replied, "Wherever I hang my hat." Levy had been employed by the playhouse, and was a roommate of Tracy in Stag Cottage. Levy claimed he went to bed at 10:45 p.m. that Saturday night, taking sleeping tablets, and woke up at 1:30 a.m. He saw Tracy sitting on the bed, head in his hands, drunk. Levy helped him take off his shirt and climb into bed. Levy said Tracy was still in bed at 4:00 a.m.

Levy admitted on cross-examination that his memory was bad. He had no recollection that their roommate, Everett Moll, had pinched Levy's feet to wake him, but was unsuccessful. Moll had said Tracy drove off at quarter to two.

Volpe tried to introduce evidence that Tracy had both motive and opportunity to commit the murder, but the judge denied his request because, as he had already stated, the case was not about Tracy.

Closing arguments took an hour for each side. Volpe faced the jury. "I know you must be pretty happy to realize that we are nearing the end of this important case. I feel kind of sorry for Mr. Smith."

He said the government called twenty witnesses, and he did not disagree with any of them. If Kipp had not called the police because of the fearful look, Volpe averred that Huntingdon never would have been arrested. And had he not shown Crossley the letter from Edna White, she never would have been implicated. The letter created a culpability by Huntingdon in Crossley's mind.

Volpe pointed out four inconsistencies in Huntingdon's letter that the prosecutor overlooked: 1.) It stated that the first day of class was tomorrow, which meant Tuesday. 2.) It mentioned the opening assembly as this morning, which was Monday. 3.) Huntingdon knew nothing of the murder last night, which was Sunday. 4.) And Mrs. Smith died yesterday morning, which was Sunday.

The letter, then, had to have been composed on Monday, the day after the murder was discovered. The police had matched the letter with the wrong envelope and then accused Rice of misdating his letter. "Why gentlemen, a telephone call would have cleared this case up," said Volpe. "Now you see how easy it is to be indicted."

At the state police interrogation, Huntingdon had been under the distinct impression that his letter had been intercepted in the mail. Hence, he could not explain the discrepancy of dates. Volpe waxed sarcastic: "Clever Mr. Stokes, cute Mr. Stokes, darned clever detective. No wonder he [Rice] perspired, no wonder his hands shook. That was not fair play, gentlemen, when a man's life is at stake."

Volpe concluded, "I don't think there is another case in the history of the Commonwealth and this country of a man charged with murder on such evidence as has been presented in this case."

In his closing statement, Smith continued to claim the letter was Huntingdon's admission of guilt, but then added that White should have raised the issue of the letter, which could have prevented the trial. Because Huntingdon hung a "do not disturb" sign on his bedroom door, Smith claimed that was premeditation. He stated, "This crime was perpetrated in a manner with the queerness that you have heard so much about, in a paroxysm of sex rage."

District Attorney Crossley flew in that morning for closing arguments, which concluded at 10:26 a.m. on Wednesday, October 9, then left the island before the verdict was delivered.

The jury went into deliberation. The judge left the courthouse for a breath of air. Forty-five minutes later, the jury returned, and there was an anxious delay until the judge could be located.

Walter Flanders, jury foreman, handed the verdict to the clerk to read. "Ralph Huntingdon Rice, on direction of the court it is ordered that you be discharged of these indictments and to depart herewith without delay."

Family and friends surrounded Rice. He threw his arms around the shoulders of his attorneys and posed for photographers, a wide grin across his face.

Headlines of the *Gazette* proclaimed: "Jury Find Rice Not Guilty; Verdict Reached 45 Minutes After Nine Day Trial Closes." It marked the close of the first murder trial on the island.

Huntingdon made his case to the press. "I have only felt that when I could tell my story in court and explain the discrepancies there would be no question of my eventual release." He went on, "I want to express my unbounded gratitude to my faithful friends on the Island who have stood by me through thick and thin, especially to the *Vineyard Gazette* for the fair and unbiased accounts of all events since that terrible night of June 30."

In a curious way, everything worked out for Huntingdon. He gained weight in jail, his sleeping improved and his general demeanor was more relaxed.

HAPPY AFTER ACQUITTAL
Ralph Huntingdon Rice, left, and his attorney, Frank G. Volpe, after the Dukes county jury had returned its "not guilty" verdicts yesterday.

Huntingdon's exuberance at the verdict was unmatched by his attorney, Frank Volpe (right). *Courtesy of the Martha's Vineyard Museum.*

The Trial of Ralph Huntingdon Rice

After ten days of being sequestered, the jury was eager to go home. One juror, Walter Besse, was heard to cry out, "Now I'm going to have all the bananas I want!"

The trial proved to be the most expensive case in Dukes County history. Total expenses reached $8,500. The transcript had to be typed daily on onionskin pages, with double carbon paper, which required two typists. Stenography fees proved the largest single expense, upward of $2,500. Jurors were paid $6 per day. The county was not responsible for the defense, which was handled by Huntingdon Rice and his family. Over eleven hundred pages of testimony were amassed.

Henry Hough editorialized:

> *With the acquittal of Ralph Huntingdon Rice by a jury of his peers, the Vineyard's first murder trial of modern times becomes a curious passage in our annals.*
>
> *When time has softened the outlines of the trial just closed, those interested in such things will look back upon it with no little fascination. Presumably the defense might have been content with meeting the representations of the government, which were based chiefly upon a discrepancy between the date of a letter and the postmark on an envelope. But Mr. Rice's counsel chose, rather, to go further and to indicate affirmatively who the real murderer might be.*
>
> *That the mystery has not been solved is cause for great regret, and it is to be hoped that further investigation may be pursued and the solution found. It seems possible, still, that the police may arrive at the truth.*
>
> *It is impossible to doubt that after that atrocious murder, a piece of violence striking suddenly and by a chance foreign to the Vineyard's whole history, the Island returned to the peace which has characterized it so long and will characterize it in the future.*

Life did go on. Harold Tracy was returned to Barnstable to serve out his sentence for carrying a concealed weapon.

The Red Sox ended the season in fifth place. The Cincinnati Reds beat the Tigers in the World Series. Detroit's Hank Greenberg won the Most Valuable Player award, and Cleveland's Bob Feller was named the ace pitcher and player of the year. Joe DiMaggio led the league in batting at .352, with Ted Williams a close second at .344. For the Red Sox it was, "Wait till next year."

An editorial from that long-ago October praised preservation of rail service. "It begins to look as if the long arm of national defense had reached out to save the railroad line upon which Martha's Vineyard has long

The trial transcript filled hundreds of pages, yet the trial itself never resolved who killed Mrs. Smith. *Photo by the author.*

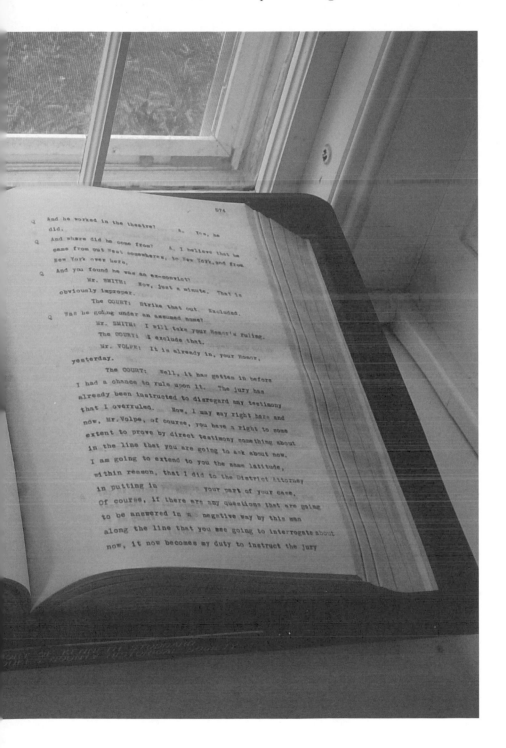

574

Q   And he worked in the theatre?   A.   Yes, he
did.

Q   And where did he come from?   A.   I believe that he
came from out West somewhere, to New York, and from
New York over here.

Q   And you found he was an ex-convict?
        Mr. SMITH: Now, just a minute.   That is
obviously improper.

        The COURT: Strike that out.   Excluded.

Q   Was he going under an assumed name?
        Mr. SMITH: I will take your Honor's ruling.
        The COURT: I exclude that.
        Mr. VOLPE: It is already in, your Honor,
yesterday.

        The COURT: Well, it has gotten in before
I had a chance to rule upon it.   The jury has
already been instructed to disregard any testimony
that I overruled.   Now, I may say right here and
now, Mr. Volpe, of course, you have a right to some
extent to prove by direct testimony something about
in the line that you are going to ask about now.
I am going to extend to you the same latitude,
within reason, that I did to the District Attorney
in putting in   your part of your case.
Of course, if there are any questions that are going
to be answered in a   negative way by this man
along the line that you are going to interrogate about
now, it now becomes my duty to instruct the jury

depended. We refer to the Old Colony line from Boston to Woods Hole."
The Flying Dude had been one of the deluxe trains on the line.

The *Gazette* was packed with news of the war. "Now comes Camp Edwards
to the Cape, with a fever of activity and a branch railroad to be built across
to the Camp itself. Of all this the Vineyard will be the beneficiary." Even
with fears of war with Hitler, Hough found a silver lining.

A letter writer protested the army's plan to take over the Oak Bluffs Trade
Winds airport, worrying that it was too near town and would disrupt the
peace of abutters.

And on the world stage, Hitler postponed Operation Sealion. The British
had proven too determined to surrender.

A cheerful correspondent commented about waving amicably when he
passed two cars on the Merritt Parkway in New York. One had a Vineyard
emblem in the window and the other bore an insignia of the *Vineyard
Gazette*. Why the wave? "Because of that Vineyard magic that draws us back
year after year—a bit of old New England—the wide expanses of sea and
sky—companionships of old friends and new—all that makes the Vineyard
lovable. We recognized each other as grains of the same old sand-pile,"
wrote John Del Mar.

The temperature settled in the fifties and low sixties during that second
week of October, dipping to a low of thirty-eight in early October. With
Crossley off island in the throes of a tight election campaign, Assistant
District Attorney Frank Smith announced he had no immediate plans for
further indictments in the Clara Smith case.

chapter seven
THE WINTER OF 1941

Though the number was below expectations, over five hundred Vineyard men registered for the draft on October 16, 1940. A few indicated they were conscientious objectors, either on religious or ethical grounds, and thus refused to bear arms.

The 1940 Oak Bluffs town directory praised high school physical education teacher William McConnor for improvements in the physical fitness of Oak Bluffs students. Townspeople had regretted the high number of military service rejections during the First World War and were impressed Mr. McConnor raised the standards in preparation for the United States' involvement in the impending war.

Duck hunting proved very successful on opening day, October 15, according to game warden Gordon Spofford. Based on early reports, bluebills and blackbills were most numerous.

Actor James Cagney returned to California after several weeks at his Chilmark home. He cherished his time on the Vineyard and, as the *Gazette* rhapsodized, "The Island knows that inwardly Jimmie is happiest when he puts on his dungarees and gets out with his horses and dogs among the Island hills." Not long after his return to Hollywood, Cagney phoned Sergeant Altieri of the state police with a request for an airmail delivery of native scallops and quahogs.

The Island Theatre in Oak Bluffs screened *Black Friday*, which starred Boris Karloff and Bela Lugosi.

Artist Thomas Hart Benton of Chilmark painted a portrait of a British sailor returning home after months at sea. In the painting, the sailor stares in awe at the city of London, sandbagged against German air raids.

The thermometer tumbled below freezing in late October. Low-lying regions of the island dipped into the low twenties. Autumn flowers wilted and birdbaths froze. It was an abrupt end to Indian summer.

District Attorney Crossley announced the engagement of his daughter Marion. In addition to the loss of his case against Huntingdon Rice, he was also soundly defeated in the election for attorney general by Robert Bushnell, although he retained his elected position as district attorney. He indicated no intent to retry the murder case.

With the trial over, Henry Hough turned to the changing seasons and national defense. But a letter to the editor kept the story of the murder alive. Herbert Hail Taylor, a criminologist, praised the *Gazette* for its unyielding effort to present the unvarnished truth, unlike the Boston papers.

At the end of December, two Vineyarders were drafted to meet the current quota. Many more faced conscription if they didn't voluntarily enlist. The United States was preparing for war.

In his year-end editorial, Hough returned to the crime. Under "Unfinished Business," he referred to "the black spot of last summer's unsolved murder," and considered the trial itself pointless. He railed that for all intents and purposes the case was dropped, although he believed there was sufficient cause to revisit it.

Hough said police had had sufficient evidence to charge the true culprit, Harold Tracy. He blamed Captain Stokes and his state police detectives for overzealous efforts to pin the charges on Huntingdon Rice. In an aside he wondered if the police were embarrassed by errors of their investigation, and then remonstrated them for allowing their prime suspect to get away with murder.

Evidence had been introduced in the trial that deserved explanation. Hough hinted that authorities had strong suspicions as to who the murderer was. "Before it is too late," he challenged the district attorney, "we hope that the good name of the Vineyard and the interests of justice will be served by an investigation as vigorous and as unprejudiced as possible."

Other news Vineyarders perused in the last week of 1940 included an earthquake that caused dishes to rattle, pictures to sway and beds to shake across the Vineyard.

A bottle found on Little Beach in Edgartown had been tossed into New York Harbor fifteen months earlier by a man from Buffalo.

Low water level in ponds and the lack of acorns presaged a mild winter. Norman Benson noted now there was not even a skim of ice on Uncle Seth's Pond in West Tisbury, but last year he had driven his car across the pond before Christmas.

A pedestrian was slightly injured when he was hit by a car while walking home from the late boat, after singing in Falmouth with a group known as the Pine Ridge Boys. George Fisher Pease suffered minor injuries and was reprimanded by local constables for walking with traffic, rather than facing it.

Army engineers surveyed the promontory of Peaked Hill for an observation point and radar station to detect enemy ships and submarines.

In early February, Hough again challenged the district attorney. "We believe the atrocious murder of Mrs. Smith is a vital public concern which should have the earnest attention of the detective branch of the state police force." Why not make the truth plain, "so plain that the terrible crime shall not remain a reproach and a mystery," Hough queried.[15]

And in a personal letter to Crossley in March 1941, Hough recounted specific facts he felt should be investigated. This letter compiled the most comprehensive and compelling evidence against Harold Tracy. The letter made the following points:

1.) Tracy was employed as an electrician by the playhouse and was very familiar with the premises. He had carried Mrs. Smith's bags to her room when she first arrived. Tracy was enamored of Marjorie Massow, and was having an affair with her. They had a signal. When Massow left the window shade of her third-floor room halfway down, Tracy was to come up. In his inebriated state on that fateful night, Tracy only got as far as the second floor. Tracy was angered and confused at finding himself in bed with the wrong woman; he violently raped and then killed Mrs. Smith.

2.) Tracy's roommates confirmed he was intoxicated when he drove off in the beach wagon. They testified his intent to find a woman, any woman.

3.) The jail matron assumed that the police knew Tracy admitted he found himself on the stairs of Sumner Hall in the early morning hours of June 30, 1940, unable to explain how he got there.

4.) When he was arrested for the concealed weapon, Tracy's trousers were damp. He claimed he washed his own clothes. The inference was that Tracy washed the blood from his clothes.

5.) Tracy had an alibi with acquaintances to cover for him. When he was arrested, Tracy threatened suicide.

6.) Hough personally considered Tracy capable of committing such a heinous crime.

Hough reiterated that the public deserved justice. "I am writing at this time," he concluded, "because of the fact that I know further steps, to be successful, must be taken immediately, and that the month of April will be too late. If it is desired to summon these witnesses, they can be located."

Hough's letter had the desired effect. The district attorney requested the judge reconvene the grand jury. The case would be retried. Indictments would be handed down. The wheels of justice would shift into high gear once more. All signs pointed to an indictment against Harold Tracy, who was still in custody at the Barnstable House of Correction on the concealed weapons charge. It looked like justice would finally and fairly be served.

Harold Tracy did not wait around for an engraved invitation.

Between four and five in the afternoon of Saturday, April 19, 1941, Harold Tracy climbed a ladder in a hallway of the jail, picked a lock in a ceiling hatch and pushed through to freedom. He hurried across the roof, dropped a dozen feet to another roof—where he bruised his ribs—and shimmied down a chimney to the ground.

Initial reports in the *Cape Cod Standard Times* indicated footprints were found nearby. Tracy scurried along railroad tracks to avoid detection. The newspaper noted Tracy was thirty-eight years old and stood five feet ten inches, with a dark complexion, narrow features and wavy, dark brown hair.

The *Gazette* picked up the chase. After a full account of the escape the reporter wrote ominously, "He is still at large." Henry Hough was dumbfounded. "The escape of Harold Tracy from the Barnstable House of Correction adds one more amazing sequence to the strange events of the Smith murder case. That Tracy should have taken French leave, without any apparent difficulty, just about ten days before the convening of the grand jury at Edgartown, is extraordinary to say the least."

It was an outrage, Hough harangued. "It will remain a reproach to those charged with the administration of justice that a figure so concerned in an unsolved murder case should have escaped so easily. There is a grave burden resting upon these officials as to what they will do now." Hough threw down the gauntlet, but the district attorney could not pick it up.

Even as he broke out of jail, Harold Tracy exhibited a modicum of manners. He penciled an exculpatory letter to his jailer, George Barker, ostensibly to ease pressure on him. "I hate to run out on you like this, but after all it is the only thing I can do."

Tracy was disingenuous. In his letter to Massow the previous summer, he had tried to throw the police off his trail. Now, in April 1941, he pointedly avoided any mention of the pending indictment from Oak Bluffs.

Tracy wrote,

> *As things now stand, if I were turned over to Kentucky I wouldn't have a chance of an acquittal on the charges against me. I hope you will not feel yourself to blame in the least for my escape. If I hadn't gone from here I would have gone from downstairs. I could have left at any time since last July but I kept putting it off in hopes I could get someone to intercede for me in Kentucky, but I can't wait any longer.*
>
> *I don't mind serving time for something of which I am guilty, but I'll be damned if I'll serve time for a crime someone else committed and blamed onto me to save their own dirty hide, knowing that my previous record would convict me.*
>
> *When I've done that, I'll return here and finish my sentence with any additional sentence the court may impose upon me for my escape, but in doing that, I will be serving for something I did and not for something I was blamed for.*
>
> *I tried to leave things in as good condition as possible. Best of luck and hoping to see you when everything is straightened out. I remain, sincerely, Tracy.*

Tracy was the first prisoner to escape from the Barnstable jail, which opened in 1935. The sheriff knew most of the inmates and trusted them. It was not unusual to allow an inmate to go to the store for the sheriff or run errands as necessary. Tracy took advantage of a lax situation, and made the most of it.

Details leaked out about his escape. Tracy managed to dye his clothes to look like a railroad worker and made a sledgehammer out of cardboard to perfect the disguise. Earlier, he had been asked to perform electrical work that required a key to the scuttle, which he never returned. It was two hours before he was discovered missing.

With a hidden twenty-dollar bill, Tracy limped into town. He made three attempts before he found a shop clerk willing and able to make change. Tracy took a taxi to Middleboro, another to Boston and then hopped a train for New York. He hid out in a cheap hotel until his ribs healed, then boarded a train for Chicago.

At the end of April the grand jury convened on the murder case. George Barker, the identification specialist from Barnstable House of Correction, was called, as were Betty and Henry Hough and the jailer's wife, Mrs.

Nathan Mercer. District Attorney William Crossley told the *New Bedford Standard Times*, "There are certain matters I wanted to present before the Grand Jury." On May 11, 1941, the grand jury indicted Tracy, in absentia, on the murder, rape and robbery of Clara Smith.

Phidelah Rice recovered enough by the spring of 1941 to take a more active role in his enterprises. He sought to publicly distance himself from Harold Tracy. In a letter printed in the *Gazette*, Rice wrote that his school did not employ Tracy, who had worked for the playhouse under an assumed name. That did nothing to rectify the situation. Tracy was a fugitive. Both the Rice School and Playhouse shuttered their doors. Later in the year Phidelah suffered a relapse and his health continued to decline from his undisclosed illness.

In an undated letter to Henry Hough from Charles Emerson Cook, the playhouse manager wrote,

> *I had a pathetic letter from Ralph Rice recently, from Boston, hoping I would steer him toward some employment. But the dread finger is upon him, and the only advice I can give is that he cut clear of all connections in the east and go back to Colorado with his sister, where he might have a new deal. He was a little resentful because Mrs. Rice had informed him there would be no place for him next summer. But she cannot be blamed. They will have a tough enough time as it is to rehabilitate the school after all that happened last summer.*

And in a plaintive letter to Hough, Huntingdon pleaded for compensation for false arrest. He implied Tracy had an accomplice to furnish money and disguise to make good his escape.

Huntingdon sought requital from the Commonwealth for the egregious treatment he suffered and claimed he was unable to find work because of the trial. He beseeched Hough to continue the cause. "I shall not soon forget your sterling loyalty to me, a man you scarcely know."

Hough promptly responded, but the letter was returned, unopened. Huntingdon left town without a forwarding address.

In late 1941, Huntingdon's defense attorney Frank Volpe, now assistant attorney general, moved beyond Huntingdon to make a name for himself in the Commonwealth. He revived indictments against reputed mob boss Raymond Patriarca for possession of firearms and burglary tools.

Assistant Defense Attorney Alfred Walton wrote to Hough early in 1942. Walton lamented that "poor Rice tries constantly to spur the State Police into some effort to locate Tracy. I feel, however, his apprehension would be embarrassing to too many officials, and that the Vineyard's murder must remain one of those things that is unsolved."

Phidelah Rice never fully recovered from the illness that debilitated him in the spring of 1940. On March 17, 1944, he died in his Brookline home, with his wife and daughter at his side. He was only sixty-two, but he had lived a very productive life. It was noted in his obituary that his Vineyard ventures were closed due to the war. No mention was made of the murder.

Besides Elizabeth and Carolee, Phidelah was survived by his sister May and brothers Bernard and Huntingdon. The latter was a resident of New York City, a man of musical interests. (When Bernard died in 1949, Huntingdon was listed as living in San Francisco; this was the last known address for him.)[16]

Carolee married and settled down, first in the western part of the state and later in Connecticut when her husband was transferred. They raised four children. The eldest, Susan Canha, moved back to the Vineyard, where she in turn raised her family.[17]

The Rice School and the Playhouse closed, whether due to the murder or because of the turmoil of the war. The buildings were hidden beneath the leafy scrub oak and pine needles of East Chop.

After Phidelah died, Elizabeth Rice sold the properties on East Chop. First to go was land that abutted Morton Park in the Highlands, in early 1948. In August of 1951 the Club House was sold to Mr. and Mrs. Carlton Knight and torn down. They built a new summer home on the site, overlooking Nantucket Sound. Elizabeth Rice sold the West Dormitory in Sumner Park in the mid-1950s and then signed papers on the imposing, sprawling family home on Arlington Street.[18]

The playhouse reopened under different management for summer productions from 1948 through 1954. Then it closed for good and was sold to the East Chop Beach Club in November 1955. The Beach Club also purchased, and later razed, the three-story, weather-shingle dormitory Sumner Hall. All that remains of the scene of the crime is the seaside stone foundation.

Secluded beneath the scrub pines of East Chop, this stately summer estate was the hub of the Rice household in the summer of 1940. *Photo by the author.*

This feeble foundation is all that remains of the once imposing Sumner Hall dormitory. *Photo by the author.*

An FBI agent recognized Harold Tracy from a wanted poster in Chicago and he was arrested without incident on October 28, 1942. Tracy had been on the run for eighteen months. Once again, it looked like justice would be served.

Tracy was returned to Louisville, Kentucky, and sentenced to the federal penitentiary in Lewisburg, Pennsylvania, for unlawful flight to avoid prosecution for his part in the jewelry robbery in Owensboro, Kentucky, in 1937. Hough noted dryly, "He had considerable unfinished business."

Six months later, in April of 1943, he was brought back to Massachusetts to face the jailbreak charge from Barnstable and was sentenced to eight to ten years in Charleston Prison, but was remanded back to Lewisburg, apparently to serve the sentences concurrently. The jailbreak sentence was reduced. Grand jury indictments loomed ahead.

The year 1943 was the height of the world war. The focus of the Vineyard, indeed the whole country, was on what was happening on two fronts overseas. The murder on East Chop diminished in significance.

To successfully charge Tracy, Hough observed, "The police would have had to turn up what they never had been able to find: incriminating fingerprints, blood stains, or the watch, brooch, and ring taken from the room at Sumner Hall." He noted, "The case had staled and could not be made fresh again."

On August 17, 1944, the *New Bedford Standard Times* announced the abrupt resignation of District Attorney William Crossley. "The District Attorney's office had been under investigation by the Attorney General," the paper reported. As Crossley left a brief meeting with the attorney general, he said, "'I've resigned.' He was visibly shaken," the reporter noted.

Attorney General Robert Bushnell issued a statement: "This resignation follows several months of investigation which I considered it the duty of the Attorney General to undertake. It makes unnecessary any further proceedings against the resigning District Attorney."

Crossley, a native of Fall River, had graduated from Boston University Law School in 1914 and been a partner in a local law firm. He served in the state legislature prior to winning election as district attorney of the Southern

Tracy to Be Arraigned Tomorrow In Barnstable for Jail Escape

HAROLD TRACY

Harold Tracy, 37, who escaped two years ago today from Barnstable Jail, where he was serving a year sentence for carrying a concealed weapon, and since then has been indicted for the murder of Mrs. Clara M. Smith, 70, at Oak Bluffs, will be arraigned in Barnstable Superior Court tomorrow morning, District Attorney William C. Crossley announced last night.

The former fugitive, held in the Federal prison at Lewisburg, Pa., since last November, is being brought back to the Cape on a habeas corpus writ to answer a jailbreaking indictment, Mr. Crossley said.

Mr. Crossley added that plans have been made to have Tracy before Dukes County Superior Court at Edgartown April 27 to face arraignment on the murder indictment pending there.

Free Two Years

Federal authorities honored the habeas corpus writ which Superior Judge Joseph Walsh approved in

(Continued on Page 2)

April 1943

Harold Tracy claimed he was "a public scapegoat" at a hearing for sentence reduction on the jailbreak charge. The eight- to ten-year sentence was reduced to three to five. *Courtesy of the Martha's Vineyard Museum.*

District in 1927. He lost the election for attorney general in 1940, but won reelection as district attorney for another term.

The then-current Assistant Attorney General Frank Volpe, Huntingdon's defense attorney, pointedly remarked, "It is too bad that the Attorney General's office is obliged to come down here to do the work the District Attorney is obliged to do." His remarks were in reference to fifty-three indictments against people whom Crossley had never arraigned. In many cases bench warrants had not even been issued. Furthermore, fewer than ten of seventy people indicted by a New Bedford Grand Jury had ever been brought to trial. Incompetence was the general consensus and the *Standard Times* wondered if the Bristol Bar Association should take up the matter.

The *Standard Times* stated, "In light of the fact that this investigation impelled Mr. Crossley to resign, it is a fair inference that it disclosed a serious situation in his conduct of his office."

Governor Leverett Saltonstall named Frank Smith of Taunton, current assistant district attorney, to fill the unexpired two years of Crossley's term as district attorney. This was the same Frank Smith who had unsuccessfully prosecuted the case against Huntingdon Rice in 1940.

In early 1945, Smith was notified that Harold Tracy would return to Massachusetts to face the murder charge.

Hough wondered, "Whether a trial would be feasible in any event, under wartime conditions, seems dubious." On the front page of that January 26, 1945 *Gazette*, Hough expounded.

> *Meanwhile, however, the case continues as complicated and confusing to laymen as it has been since Tracy himself spun a tortuous web by seeking sanctuary on the Vineyard, becoming involved in a murder, going to Barnstable on a year's sentence for illegal possession of a dangerous weapon, escaping from jail, and getting caught by the F.B.I. in Chicago. The problem of finding witnesses would probably be a hard one.*

Even the persistent Hough seemed resigned to let the case slide into history.

Edgartown High School's history and sociology students were in court on April 30, 1946, to witness legal proceedings. District Attorney Smith was in charge of the cases being prosecuted. Judge Walter Collins presided.

A man with the same name as the district attorney was allowed to go free, although he admittedly broke into a number of Oak Bluffs cottages. Frank Smith was a decorated war veteran, but the court felt he needed mental health treatment more than a prison sentence.

Then, with the "Court quietly agog," Harold Tracy was brought in by Sheriff Lauchlan Crocker of Barnstable County. "Tracy, dapper and deferential, with no trace of prison pallor, had recently been in Norfolk Prison Colony," reported the *Gazette*.

Smith told the court he was not satisfied that Tracy was guilty of murder, nor should he be put on trial. Then the district attorney nol-prossed the complaints in the court records; in effect, he dropped all charges.

The *Gazette* reported Tracy's reaction. "Tracy, thanking the judge, evidently unable to believe that he would be permitted to leave the courtroom unescorted, looked from one officer to another, and then noting their assent to his unspoken question, walked quietly from the courtroom," Harold Tracy was a free man.

Hough editorialized on the status of the case in the *Gazette* of May 3, 1946: "With the freeing of Harold Tracy by the Superior Court on Tuesday, the atrocious Island murder of 1940 slips away into the annals of unsolved crimes." He reminded readers that Tracy had been kept as the alternate defendant in the murder case, but concluded, "That the crime remains without solution and without punishment will always be the cause of deep regret."

chapter eight

SO WHO WAS HAROLD TRACY?

Harold Tracy came from Vanceburg, in Lewis County, Kentucky, a tiny town wedged between the Ohio River and the transcontinental railroad. People passed through Vanceburg on the river or the tracks; few lingered in this foothill of the Alleghenies.

Tracy was born in the old McDaniel house, a proper Victorian home with gingerbread decor in the porch eaves and a wrought-iron fence along the front lawn at 212 Second Street, the main street in Vanceburg.

His mother, Edythe Ingrim Tracy, was born in 1882, the daughter of Thomas and Edna Ingrim. Thomas Ingrim was a blacksmith who worked his way into the hardware business and ran a profitable enterprise in downtown Vanceburg. Edythe was known to have had a sweet disposition, a charitable manner and was a member of the Vanceburg Christian Church.

Tracy's father, William, was born in Ohio in 1878 and moved to Vanceburg in 1900. A hard worker and well respected in the community, William Tracy labored in a tobacco warehouse, most likely for his wife's cousin, Bill Dugan, father of a locally prominent thespian and editor.

Both Edythe and William were Methodists. They were married in Vanceburg in October 1901. Harold was born May 17, 1903, and his sister Edna two years later. As a youngster, Tracy spent time with his grandparents; indeed, he was listed in the 1910 census as a resident of the Vanceburg home of Edna and Thomas Ingrim. Soon his parents moved into their own house a mile or so up the river, in an area known as Black Oak Bottom, bottom referring to the flat plain along the riverbanks.

Tracy attended the old Vanceburg graded school and graduated from the local high school. He spoke well, some said with an accent, and was known to charm women with his words. And he wrote well, too. Two letters he

Vanceburg once was a customary stop for passengers on the Chesapeake and Ohio line, en route from Chicago to Washington. Today freight trains just blow their whistles as they sweep through. *Photo by the author.*

wrote recommend him as erudite and conscious of grammar, spelling and content.

Tracy struggled against the conformity of a strict Bible Belt background. When he could not repress his anger at the restrictions, he expressed it in teenage hijinks. He was involved in what was known as the "fracas at the cemetery," when vandals tipped over tombstones and monuments in the local graveyard. Townspeople were irate, but could not prove Tracy was involved. Another memorable escapade was when he moved cars from one street to another, right in town. Was this mischief-making, or a criminal in training?[19]

The town of Vanceburg was settled in the early days of the nineteenth century, shortly after Meriwether Lewis passed through and lent his name to the county. Kentucky supported Union forces during the Civil War, and boasted the only public Southern Union memorial to its soldiers. The economy was based on timber and tobacco, though salt mines and the bourbon highway were also nearby.

Vanceburg had little to entice Harold Tracy to remain, and he offered little in return. Like the river and the train, he didn't stay around for long.

Tracy was born in the Victorian McDaniel's house on the corner of Rowley and Second Streets. It's a block from the Victorian Rose, a diner's delight in downtown Vanceburg. *Photo by the author.*

Wherever he traveled, Tracy made an impression on the ladies with his tall, slender build and confident, self-assured manner. He charmed women but avoided men. And wherever possible, he avoided both responsibility and work.[20]

At the age of twenty, it is believed Tracy married and fathered a daughter. At the age of thirty Tracy found himself in Hammond, Indiana, involved in a carjacking. Although he let the victims keep their car, he was arrested and sentenced to ten years at Pendleton penitentiary in Terre Haute, Indiana. The warden of the prison complex would not confirm Tracy's incarceration; newspaper reports state he was paroled in 1937.

Shortly thereafter he was charged in a robbery in Owensboro, in western Kentucky, another link on his chain of crime. He had to get out of town. Tracy researched remote communities at the local library. That led him to Martha's Vineyard in the spring of 1940, where he was hired as a handyman at the Rice Playhouse.

After he broke out of the Barnstable jail in 1941, Tracy spent the war years first in New York and later Chicago, before he was apprehended. He served time for the Kentucky jewelry job and Barnstable jailbreak. On his return to

The Ohio River flows gently westward toward the Mississippi. This barge is being pushed upstream, past Vanceburg. *Photo by the author.*

Second Street is the primary thoroughfare in Vanceburg, site of the Lewis County Courthouse. *Photo by the author.*

the Vineyard in 1946 to face indictment for the murder of Clara Smith, he was acknowledged both as a seasoned criminal and as a man of the world. Through it all, or in spite of it, he retained an aura of bravado and charm that women from Vanceburg to the Vineyard found endearing.[21]

When the charges against him were dropped, Tracy made his way back to Kentucky a free man, but he never settled down for long.[22]

In the decade following Tracy's release from the Vineyard indictments, his parents showed their age. Edythe Tracy died intestate in an Ohio nursing home in April 1957 at the age of seventy-four. Harold, his father and sister Edna were named beneficiaries of her estate. At the time, Harold was in New Orleans.

For a number of years William Tracy had been in ill health. After Edythe died, he too returned to Ohio to live with his sister. When he died in May 1958, Harold was listed as a resident of Hammond, Indiana, a suburb of Chicago, where his sister, her husband Cliff MacKinnon and their five children lived. On his father's death, Harold returned to Vanceburg. Both Edythe and William Tracy are buried in the Black Oak Methodist cemetery, less than a mile from their Vanceburg home in Black Oak Bottom.

Main Street runs from the railroad tracks down to the Ohio. With a population of fewer than two thousand, there is not much activity in Vanceburg. *Photo by the author.*

In an Affidavit of Descent, filed in autumn of 1958, Harold Tracy and Edna MacKinnon were listed as heirs to their father's estate. Harold was fifty-five and Edna was two years younger. The siblings sold the property in Black Oak Bottom for $18,000. It consisted of two parcels of land, with boundary markers defined by dogwood trees and paces.

Certain conditions were listed in the agreement. Growing crops were assigned to the new owners, except for tobacco, which was to be shared between Harold and Edna. They also held the option to the milk check, expected at the end of September 1958. The siblings assumed responsibility for the taxes due at the end of the year.

Harold also retained the right to reside on the property "in a small building in the rear of the residence on this property for a period of three months from this date, but he will vacate said premises sooner if possible." In 1960, Tracy showed up in the Lewis County Courthouse to handle legal matters regarding the property out in Black Oak Bottom.[23]

A peripatetic lifestyle characterized Tracy all his days; he never worked for long and never settled down.

Harold Tracy's parents, fine, upstanding citizens, were buried in Black Oak Bottom. They lived in Vanceburg all their lives. *Photo by the author.*

In the early 1960s, Tracy left Vanceburg again, this time heading north, back to Hammond, Indiana, near his sister and her family. He settled in a rooming house that was close to his family, but not too close.

For years, Tracy suffered from emphysema, and he died on August 28, 1964, at the age of sixty-one, already an old man. Aside from his sister and her family, the only survivor listed in his obituary in the Hammond *Times Mirror* was his daughter, Betty Leonard. She had three children, Harold Tracy's grandchildren.

Tracy is interred in Section 1, Lot 23 of the Elmwood Cemetery in Hammond, Indiana. There is no headstone on his grave.

Years later, Tracy's niece Dorothy Hartog recalled her uncle. "He was a brilliant man—if only he had taken advantage of his intelligence—he could have been sitting on Easy Street all those years."

Tracy

Services for H a r o l d Thomas Tracy, 61, of 5946 Hohman Ave.. Hammond, will be Saturday at 1 p.m. in the Emmerling-Paddack Chapel, 6020 Hohman Ave.

The Rev. Harlod W. Turpin will officiate. Burial will be in Elmwood Cemetery.

Mr. Tracy died Wednesday in his apartment at the Southmoor Apartment Hotel. Survivors are a daughter, Mrs. Betty Leonard of Canton, Ohio; a siter, and three grandchildren.

The *Times of Northwest Indiana*, primary newspaper of Munster, Indiana, ran this obituary in late August 1964, complete with the misspelling. *Courtesy of Lake County Public Library.*

Was Harold Tracy guilty of the rape and murder Clara Smith?

On September 3, 1982, Henry Hough published a piece in the *Vineyard Gazette* about the murder. (The story was reprinted on September 7, 2007.)

As Hough bluntly recounted the tale, he was sitting with William Everett Moll on the porch of the Harbor View Hotel in the late summer of 1982. The conversation turned to the murder of 1940, and Hough asked Moll, "Don't you think Tracy must have been the murderer?" Moll's response was unequivocal: "I know he was. He told me so."

With those posthumous words, the saga rests.

chapter nine

WHAT WENT WRONG?

To grasp the confluence of circumstances that allowed an elderly woman to be murdered and an introverted bachelor to be charged with the crime, and set up conditions that led to the escape and eventual freedom of the perpetrator, we examine four key elements in the case. Why did Clara Smith die? How was the investigation handled? What impact did incarceration have? How did the prosecution pursue the case?

As Henry Hough would say, the case continues to amaze.

THE CRIME

Tracy was a heavy drinker. All evidence points in that direction. The night of June 29, 1940, Tracy had worked all day at the playhouse and then drove downtown and spent the evening with co-workers in the bars on Circuit Avenue.

Alcohol produces a rush when it gets into the bloodstream quickly. A rapid increase in blood alcohol concentration caused by consumption of large quantities of alcohol in a short time can induce a blackout. A blackout blocks the capacity of the participant to incorporate short-term memory into long term recollection. The participant lives for the moment, with no concept of the consequence of his actions. A blackout, which is a symptom of alcoholism, may be partial, with only fragments of an event remembered, or complete, known as en bloc, in which a whole experience is never recorded, so to speak. Fragmentary blackouts are more common.

Tracy claimed he had no knowledge of what he did that night. Alcohol can have that effect. It can interfere with one's ability to create new memories, hence the inability to recall activities. A blackout is alcohol-induced amnesia.

As opposed to passing out, blackouts do not involve a loss of consciousness. Participants can function. They can drive a car, wash the dishes, have sexual relations. Yet alcohol has an amnesiac effect, so the participant has no recollection he engaged in these activities. It is akin to a hypnotic trance in that the participant is awake and conscious, but unable to act independently in his thought process. Witnesses may be unaware the participant is in a blackout. Behavior appears routine and the participant seems to be in control of his actions. Alcohol creates a memory dysfunction.

Bruce Kerr is a clinical and forensic psychologist who practices in Maine. "Alcohol is a disinhibitor. When someone is an alcoholic, their defenses are limited or blocked, so there is no conscience or restriction on aberrant behaviors. Tracy was so drunk he had nothing to hold him back from what he wanted."

Tracy wanted a woman.

Kerr says,

> In a blackout state, a serious alcoholic can function. He is so inured to the alcoholic state that he can function almost normally, but without the restrictions of sobriety. Hence, Tracy sought sex and made his way to his girlfriend's dormitory at Sumner Hall. He went up to the room he presumed was hers.
>
> As for his attack on Mrs. Smith, we can only imagine that he was extremely angry she deceived him by not being his girlfriend. He retaliated by killing her with brute force. Again, there were no inhibitors, because he was drunk. To show his superiority, the final indignity, he raped her.
>
> In cases of an alcoholic blackout, the person may well have no recollection of the incident, even though he functioned almost rationally in his effort to carry it out.

Dr. Donal Sweeney wrote *The Alcohol Blackout: Walking Talking Unconscious & Lethal.* His book describes a blackout as an unconscious state that may last several hours or even days until the alcohol works through the system. During that time, the memory function fails. Such a condition renders the participant a danger to himself and those around him, because he is impulsive and lacks an ability to think, plan or learn from his actions.

"Alcohol blocks formation of new memory, but old memory remains," writes Dr. Sweeney. "People know their family and friends, their schooling, all the procedures they knew previously. They can walk, talk, drive, but they have no idea what happened a minute ago or what they are going to do next." The participant is helpless to control his memory function.

Lack of self-control can lead to a hostile response. The participant reacts to stimuli, unaware of consequences. This condition is known as alcohol myopia or tunnel vision.

"Self-control and decision-making disappear, along with hard-learned inhibitions. Dangers go unrecognized. Thoughts and actions are entirely impulsive." Dr. Sweeney adds, "People in a blackout are in great peril. And no one realizes it. They risk harming themselves and others. Nothing less than death and ruined lives may be at stake."

Karen Franklin, PhD, has written on the forensic implications of alcoholic blackouts. "It is not uncommon for someone arrested for a serious offense to claim that he or she does not remember what happened. Often, the basis of the claimed amnesia is an alcohol blackout."

She explained, "An alcohol blackout is an amnesia for significant events that occurred during a drinking episode, when at the time the person's behavior might not have appeared disordered." Franklin added,

> *Forensic psychologists have specialized methods to assist in determining when a person might be feigning a mental disorder or a memory deficit, including an alcohol blackout. Criminal defendants do not realize that being in a blackout state does not necessarily excuse their crime. A blackout just relates to one's later memory of what happened. While in a blackout, a person may still be able to recognize whether their behavior is right or wrong.*

A blackout, then, describes the condition whereby the participant can continue to function. In no way does it absolve the perpetrator of responsibility for his actions. It may explain why he acted as he did, but it does not excuse his behavior. A criminal act is still a criminal act.

Mike Ditchfield is a Massachusetts psychologist, living and practicing on Martha's Vineyard.

If you rape someone when drunk, it could have been that Tracy was afraid that the woman could identify him, so he killed her. Or he could have had some insane idea she wanted sex with him. In his psychotic state, it could have made sense to Tracy. And then he killed her. Tracy could have been angry at Mrs. Smith for trying to break up his romance. These people [who have blackouts] *get really crazy. Rape could have been sex, in his mind, then he got angry. He was already in a delusional state of mind. People do it all the time.*

In his blackout condition, Ditchfield says, "It almost makes sense. You hear about people who go around the world and end up in Australia and they don't know how they got there. He could have been manic. Manic people can do really crazy stuff. Drinking makes it worse. They think drinking helps, but it actually makes it worse."

Susan Brownmiller's epic, *Against Our Will. Men, Women and Rape*, covers rape-murder. Brownmiller notes national figures on rape-murder are not available because the result is homicide, and that is what is counted, not in conjunction with rape.

She recalled the 1964 Kitty Genovese case and the 1962–64 Boston strangler murders, which were highlights in the annals of crime in the latter third of the twentieth century.

Kitty Genovese was stalked on her residential Queens, New York street by Winston Moseley, who claimed he went out to find a girl and kill her. Thirty-eight people heard Miss Genovese's frantic cries for help, but no one responded. Moseley stabbed Miss Genovese and then raped her. He preferred victims unable to fight back before he raped them.

Albert DeSalvo terrorized Boston, strangling and stabbing thirteen women. DeSalvo garnered an unusual reputation in Cambridge, where he was known as the Measuring Man. He would entice a young woman to allow him into her apartment, posing as a representative of a modeling agency. Then he would measure her breasts and hips. During this same era, he assumed another identity in the western part of the state when he broke into homes and raped women. Attired in green pants, he was called the Green Man. Like Moseley, DeSalvo strangled or stabbed women prior to violating them. His first victims were older, over fifty, the eldest seventy-five. He faced less resistance from elderly women. Neither age nor attractiveness mattered. "She was a woman," said DeSalvo. "When this certain time comes on me, it's a very immediate thing." He felt power when he murdered and raped a woman.

Brownmiller referred to a study entitled "Patterns in Forcible Rape," which reported "the offender's judgment was impaired, usually by the consumption of alcohol before the event." The report observed the offender "drinks more alcohol prior to his crime than the man who goes out to rob."

Bill Talley earned his doctorate in counseling psychology. He retired to Vanceburg, Kentucky, Tracy's hometown.

"Given [Tracy's] artistic autograph and his interest in the arts [he was in the playbills in Vanceburg in the 1920s and again in the 1950s, after his stint working at the Rice Playhouse], perhaps he wanted to express himself in the arts, when he went to Martha's Vineyard."

Dr. Talley considered Tracy's background. "He probably disappointed his parents. They were quite upstanding in town. He didn't fit in. He needed a special niche."

As for the rape, Dr. Talley suggested it "represented repressed anger, anger harbored in a repressive Methodist household. The rape was an outlet for his anger. Rape can be sexual assault and is a form of abuse, an act of domination."

THE INVESTIGATION

When Oak Bluffs Police Chief Amaral arrived at Sumner Hall, he knew he had to report Mrs. Smith's death to the state police. Besides the fact that it was protocol, he also had no expertise in violent crime.

Chief Amaral fingered evidence such as the wastebasket, windowsill and bed. When an expert dusted the room, the preponderance of prints belonged to the chief. The rest of the investigation, from roping off the site to interviewing suspects, was handled appropriately.

Oak Bluffs Lieutenant Tim Williamson describes current protocol. The first officer to respond to the crime immediately secures the perimeter and initiates a logbook of who enters. "Any suspects would be apprehended and brought to the station for questioning, after being informed of their Miranda rights," said Williamson. (This was not a statute in 1940.) The first responder notifies Oak Bluffs Police Department and state police. "The Massachusetts state police detectives unit is the investigatory arm of the District Attorney's office [which] has jurisdiction in unattended deaths or deaths of a suspicious nature."

"Witnesses would be identified and questioned separately at the scene and most likely contacted for future follow-up questioning," adds Williamson.

The police detective would apply for a search warrant and, once obtained, begin an exacting search of the premises. "A team of investigators from the Cape Cod office would be brought to the island as soon as possible." This happened in 1940 as well. The team is made up of specialists who photograph the crime scene, sketch diagrams and look for and recover trace evidence. Williamson explains, "Trace evidence includes: fingerprints, weapons, shell casings, bullets and fragments, bullet trajectory, blood evidence, footprints, tire prints, tool marks, fibers, hairs, bodily fluids, clothing, DNA evidence, nature of injuries/cause of death."

Williamson would work with the "state police detectives and the district attorney's office to make a case and hopefully secure an arrest and conviction for the person/people responsible for the murder."

When we compare current protocol with how the situation was handled in 1940, we find a very similar response, even down to the professional respect and discretion shown by the officers. The major mistake in 1940 was the failure to arrest the right suspect.

London's Jack the Ripper was never apprehended. That case exposed the need for forensic science. In the latter half of the nineteenth century, Scotland Yard initiated crime scene analysis. The first forensic lab was developed in Paris in 1910 and the FBI organized one in 1932. One of the first forensic sciences was photography, which is used to document a crime scene as well as serve as a tool of the morgue.

In *Dead Reckoning*, Dr. Michael Baden and Marion Roach present an analysis of a murder investigation that begins at the end, with the autopsy, and traces the crime backward. An autopsy, writes Dr. Baden, "is to speak with and for the dead." The medical examiner should be a neutral, independent physician. In the autopsy conducted on Mrs. Smith, Dr. Buckley rendered an objective report in his court testimony.

Criminology is the examination of trace evidence that may incriminate or exclude a suspect. Criminalists reconstruct events based on patterns they uncover at the crime scene. With blood pattern analysis, criminalists read "a crime scene by the blood that was left behind and reconstruct the events as the bleeding occurred and afterward." Blood spatter analysis, based on the energy, direction and flow of blood, is key to the study of a crime scene. How blood falls, its surface tension and projectile aspects help to determine criminal activity.

A forensic pathologist determines cause of death and how it happened, but not the culprit. When a forensic pathologist testifies in court as an expert witness, he interprets the facts. His role is to synthesize information from the crime scene so the prosecutor can move the case forward.

That a weapon was never uncovered in room fifteen implies it was removed, unless it was part of the room's furnishings. This issue was virtually ignored in the trial. No one ascertained what weapon was used to fracture Mrs. Smith's skull, although a cold chisel was suggested in an early press report.

Dr. Baden says, "The basic rule of investigation: you never know what you are looking for." He observes that when forensic science is done poorly, justice suffers. "Someone is going to get away with something (murder, perhaps) or the wrong person is going to pay for another's issue." He adds, "Just how often the wrong person is arrested is nothing short of astounding. Egregious incompetence."

For a moment, let us suppose the jury had found Huntingdon Rice guilty.

How many innocent people are convicted, based on faulty evidence? The Innocence Project was founded in 1992 with a specific goal to assess cases by inmates who feel unjustly charged with a crime. False accusations range from eyewitness misidentification to forensic errors, false data, racism, false confessions and lost or tainted evidence.

DNA, or deoxyribonucleic acid, has had a major impact in determination of the guilt or innocence of suspects. Each individual's DNA is unique. Thus, trace evidence, from a cigarette butt to a plucked hair, is key to a murder investigation.

By late 2007, more than two hundred inmates had been released from prison due to DNA evidence that proved they did not commit the crime they were convicted of. DNA exoneration is "the greatest data set ever on the causes of wrongful convictions in the U.S. and yet just the tip of the iceberg," charged the Innocence Project.

Trace evidence that could have linked Tracy to the scene of the crime ranged from bloodstains on his clothes to semen on Mrs. Smith to fingerprints. He likely handled items in the room, even pushing over a wastebasket or a table. The hair grasped in her hand was evidence. Tracy could have been tied to the crime, besides intentionality and opportunity. It was all there, but was never pursued.

The evidence against Huntingdon was limited to a letter he sent to his practitioner, his "fearful look" at Lydia Kipp and excessive perspiration during his interrogation. Had he confessed to Captain Stokes on that July night, Huntingdon would have been jailed or faced the death sentence.

And he was innocent.

The Massachusetts State Police are charged with the investigation of unattended or suspicious deaths. Rick Kelley is a lieutenant with the state police.

"Forensics in the 1940s was pretty primitive. They would take fingerprints, do blood type, but relied on witness statements, time lines, motives and opportunities," says Kelley. Cold cases could be opened with technological advances, "but none of it is an exact science," he says. "You try to gather as much evidence as you can."

With over twenty-five years on the force, Kelley empathizes with the officers dispatched to Oak Bluffs in 1940. They were from the mainland, did not know anyone on the Vineyard and commuted or bunked in the barracks. In those days, "Work was 24-7, no overtime, no meal allowance. It was a military structured organization." He adds, "Chances are they put in their hours and want to get home to their families."

Regarding the evidence against Huntingdon, Kelley says, "Unless the man had facts [in the letter] that only the killer would know, it [the case against him] sounds pretty flimsy."

THE INCARCERATION

Huntingdon Rice was jailed at the Dukes County Jail and House of Correction on upper Main Street in Edgartown, which is now overseen by Sheriff Michael McCormack.

The jail was built in 1873 with twelve cells, yet was rarely full. It included quarters for the staff, as it was a live-in operation.[24] Sheriff McCormack says, "We were the last couple hired as husband and wife, back in 1973." Accommodations for inmates were primitive. "There was no indoor plumbing when I took over, so the slop bucket could become a pretty potent weapon. We got indoor plumbing pretty quick."

The cells were divided into four cellblocks with solid granite walls and thick iron-barred gates. The first block was for new admissions, and the second was likely where Huntingdon was housed. Tracy, too, was incarcerated in the Dukes County Jail and may have been on the same block.

The worst part of incarceration is the loss of personal freedoms. Inmates lose decision-making options like when to eat, sleep, who their roommates are and much more. Sheriff McCormack says, "We watch them very closely the first seventy-two hours."

Could an inmate actually improve sleeping and eating habits in the jail, as Huntingdon Rice claimed? "Not such an odd question," says the sheriff. "Three-fourths of our inmates have an alcohol or substance abuse problem, and a quarter of those suffer from mental health issues. Once they go through withdrawal, we offer medication, diagnosis and treatment of their condition, as well as regular meals and routine sleeping."

A much smaller prison population would have suited a loner like Huntingdon, who struggled with his peace of mind and was bothered by intrusions and distractions.

The jailers, Nathan and Hattie Mercer, had to feed the inmates. They served Huntingdon the same meal they ate, so he probably dined quite well.

The jail book from 1940 lists the names of prisoners, when they came and left. It's a bit of history hidden within the walls. Records indicate the Mercers ran the jail from 1933 to 1941.

Would Sheriff McCormack ever permit an attorney to promenade his defendant before the press for an interview and photographs? Frank Volpe sought to garner support for Huntingdon that way. "I would never do it," McCormack said. "They have the right to an attorney, but I would never allow the attorney to have a press conference in public at the jail. Photographs could only be taken when the prisoner was brought to and from the court, and I have no control over that."

Sheriff Jim Cummings currently oversees the Barnstable House of Correction. He sifted through old records from his jail.

We have a Harold Tracy who was held at the Barnstable County Jail in June of 1940 and was committed to a one year sentence on July 19, 1940, for carrying a concealed weapon. He is listed as a thirty-seven-year-old white male born in Kentucky and gave an occupation as a photographer. He is also listed as a high school graduate and was sent to Barnstable from Oak Bluffs, Dukes County. His father is noted as being from Ohio and the record indicates that Tracy had two former commitments, but it does not say where.

The interesting thing is that the book he is listed in has a remarks section where the end of sentence is indicated, such as paroled, finished sentence etc. In Tracy's case there is nothing written in the remarks section and Tracy's entire entry is crossed out in red ink. I don't know what this means.

When it was explained to Sheriff Cummings that Tracy had broken out of jail, the red line made sense.

Has anyone else escaped from Barnstable? "Wayne Lewis escaped in the late 1960s by cutting the bars. In the mid-'80s two cons escaped by climbing the fence approximately twelve feet. All three were recaptured and returned to the jail. Shortly after razor wire was put on the fence and there has not been an escape since."

Would a jailer ever loan an inmate a key? "In those days inmates were used for many purposes and if one were an electrician his skills would have been used. It was a way to save money and get things done. Jail in the 1940s was much different than today. The crimes for the most part were less violent and inmates were used for many things and would be allowed to do these things both inside and outside the jail without supervision."

Sheriff Cummings notes that his predecessor, Lauchlan Crocker, served as sheriff from 1933 to 1947. Lauchlan Crocker was remembered for his efforts to construct the new jail, instituting a police radio system and founding the Barnstable County Police School, which was attended by police from across the Cape.

Each inmate handles incarceration his own way. Huntingdon Rice adapted to the routine of wholesome meals, a normal sleeping schedule and a minimum of interruptions. He blossomed behind bars because he was removed from the distractions of summer life on Martha's Vineyard. For an introverted loner, the incarceration may have actually contributed to his well-being.

What Went Wrong?

Harold Tracy served time in jails from Indiana to Pennsylvania to Massachusetts. He worked the system with his outgoing manner and probably sought out an essential role to fill behind bars, as his experience in Barnstable showed. To befriend his jailer to the point of writing a letter of apology for breaking out speaks to a clever and conniving, as well as considerate, criminal.

Tracy was a slippery character, quick to blame someone else for his misdeeds. He must have begrudged getting caught, but then felt no remorse when he committed his next illegal activity.

THE PROSECUTION

Cape Cod and the Islands' District Attorney Michael O'Keefe discussed his role as prosecutor of homicide investigations. O'Keefe has served as district attorney since 1980 and prosecuted dozens of homicides. His investigations are conducted according to a tried and true methodology, "successfully replicated across the Commonwealth."[25]

In midsummer 1940, the *News of New York* rhetorically asked why Crossley acted so rashly against Rice, yet permitted Tracy to avoid prosecution. Crossley, "who is in the full heat of a political campaign for State Attorney General, has proceeded too fast," chastised the *News*. The implication was that Crossley was more intent on his election than on arresting the right suspect.

O'Keefe says, "You can't assume politics was behind his efforts. All district attorneys have to run for office. Crime doesn't stop when there's an election." He added that newspapers know only half the story. "With all due respect, I'm not impressed with what I read in the newspapers."

Crossley was actively involved in the arrest of Huntingdon Rice. O'Keefe says, "I know nothing about the case. Only since the 1970s was there a statute that the DA is in charge of homicide investigations, with the Massachusetts state police assigned to take charge." He explained that "in 1940 it was not as sophisticated [as today]; other resources would be utilized."

O'Keefe characterized the difference between evidence and speculation. A good investigator, he says, "needs to deal with the facts. Convictions are interested in the facts only. When people base something only on a political agenda their theories are conspiratorial and unfounded." Speculation has no place in the conviction of criminals.

Interestingly, he observes that if the only piece of evidence available was the letter Huntingdon mailed to Edna White, or if information had been leaked and Huntingdon was aware of it, that could be sufficient cause to consider Huntingdon a suspect and pursue a more intense interrogation. Furthermore, because Huntingdon exhibited characteristics of a loner and admittedly did not get along with women, O'Keefe feels those traits would attract the attention of the police. Perhaps Crossley was not that far off.

O'Keefe is more cautious on the subject of motive. "Motive is a funny thing. It is not part of the government burden of proof. People's motives are unfathomable for a number of things. We can't prove motive—why someone killed someone. We prove intentionality—did you do it on purpose or was it an accident?"

He adds, "Motive is great parlor conversation, but it is not always pertinent. A good investigation deals with mundane methodologies to elicit the facts. Who did what? It's very boring, but it's how we catch them."

In a follow-up interview with Sheriff Cummings, the topic of homicide investigations came up. What about circumstantial evidence? "I always found to succeed in a homicide, you need a preponderance of circumstantial evidence. Best, of course, is an eyewitness and factual evidence, but you go with what you have."

What about a motive? "It's always good to have a motive at a trial. Jurors want to know why someone would do it. By that time [of trial] you know so much about the person, you know their motive."

Sheriff Cummings rebutted the contention that Harold Tracy had suffered a blackout. "I don't buy it. They know something is bad, so they shouldn't do it. I never liked a blackout. It's too much of a perfect opportunity. Something that violent, they could recall. I think it's a phony excuse."

Liza Williamson is clerk/magistrate of the Edgartown District Court. As a former prosecutor as well as a defense attorney, she is eminently qualified to offer her opinion on the case.

She feels Tracy subconsciously knew Clara Smith was in the room he entered that fateful night, and he intended to kill her. "If there was hearsay, and Tracy knew the victim, that could account for his rage. It makes the crime a lot less random if she was one of the people in particular who frowned on them dating. It was in his subconscious, that's what I believe. Otherwise, it would be a huge coincidence."

"Rape is a crime of violence," she adds. "Control and violence, not sexual." In an aside, Williamson says, if Tracy had wanted sex, he would have gone up to his girlfriend's room on the third floor.

Regarding the district attorney, Williamson says, "It behooved him to go before the grand jury with the indictment against Harold Tracy for murder in April 1941, even based on circumstantial evidence. Two examples of such are footprints in the snow and mail in the mailbox. You didn't see the person, but there is evidence that shows someone was there. And there certainly was a preponderance of evidence that linked Harold Tracy to the crime."

Williamson notes the limits on prosecutors are clearly defined. They must lie within the rules of evidence in a criminal procedure and follow ethical standards set out for prosecutors, which are higher than for average attorneys. Prosecutors are held to a very high standard, especially in closing arguments. They must not step over the line. Court oversight ensures the DA doesn't cross the ethical line.

Under rules of criminal procedure, police must provide the defendant with any evidence that could exculpate him. And because the district attorney is an elected position, it is possible corruption or unethical practices may interfere with the high standards of prosecutors. That's why Liza Williamson is pleased that judges are not elected in Massachusetts. It keeps them focused on their jobs, without having to worry about the electorate.

Kelley, of the state police, assesses the role of the prosecution. Had there been a new trial once Huntingdon was found not guilty, Kelley says that with a new suspect, as was anticipated in the spring of 1941, "it's difficult to prosecute a second person. Looks like their theory darts around. The police weren't sure. That's why you have to present a solid case to the grand jury."

He adds that people are aware of what was said in the first trial, which might taint opinions offered in the second trial. "Sounds like they were quick to judge," says Kelley. "Goes to the character of the investigator. Did the DA put pressure on Stokes for a quick arrest?" That would have put Captain Stokes in an untenable position if he felt he had to deliver a suspect to Crossley, even with insufficient evidence. If he didn't make a quick arrest, he might have faced demotion or a transfer. It may have been a very real threat.

Kelley puts the onus of misdirection on the prosecutor. "The DA could have pressured his police to come up with a quick arrest as he was running for elected office. If the DA were a little unethical, or he wants an arrest because there's an election coming, he might push for the arrest. Make an arrest, make headlines and then release him after the election in December."

Kelley continues, "If the police know something that could exonerate the suspect, you have to look at the issue of doubt. If you don't let the grand jury know there's a question, that's unethical."

He spoke to the heart of the matter. It's human nature, says Kelley, "for someone who's unscrupulous to take this route. Integrity and ethics. You don't know someone's character." Sometimes the bad guy is in charge.

Kelley considers the role of the state police. "Even today the DA wants state police officers with him he can trust." He handpicks the officers he wants in his office, which builds a strong allegiance to the district attorney.

"O'Keefe is one of the best prosecutors. Very ethical," Kelley says. "He couldn't understand someone doing it, if it wasn't ethical. He's very competent. He surrounds himself with competent people. Top-notch team. One step at a time. Cover all the bases."

The fact that the attorney general had to demand Crossley's resignation in 1944, due to incompetence, explains why O'Keefe does not accept Crossley's responsibility in the prosecution. O'Keefe is a capable prosecutor; Crossley was inept, or at least he was toward the end of his tenure.

Another issue Kelley considers was that the jail matron, Hattie Mercer, failed to report Tracy's confession to the police. That breakdown of communication and cooperation within law enforcement ranks was critical in the prosecution of the case. Kelley nods knowingly, "Bet it was the defense that got her to testify about Tracy's statement." It was.

Kelley straddles the line between Cummings and O'Keefe on the matter of motive. Kelley considers motive a tool for the investigator. "Who had an ax to grind? Was [the murder] sexual, financial, anger, spur of the moment, or a romance gone wrong?"

Crime scene analysis can turn up a motive. If an expensive watch is found on the victim, for example, that would rule out robbery. Did the suspect know the victim? "Anger and passion are usually directed at friend or family," he adds.

Kelley agrees with O'Keefe that you suspect "evidentiary actors" to determine who had the intent to commit the crime. But he also considers motive, because it helps guide the investigation. It sends you in the right direction, he says.

Like Cummings, Kelley doesn't agree with the blackout concept. "I don't buy it. If he's that drunk, he's not going to get an erection. I'm more inclined to think: she recognized him, he killed her to cover up the crime. There was not much in forensics—kill the witness, you get a home run. Difficult to prosecute." He wraps the case with the confidence of an experienced professional.

With forensic evidence ranging from fingerprints to DNA, one might assume police solve every murder that comes along. Not so. Literally thousands of murders go unsolved each year. In the FBI Uniform Crime Report of 2004, over 60 percent of homicides were considered resolved, which means nearly 40 percent were still open.

Based on homicides per 100,000 population, with a constant of 37.4 percent, the rate of uncleared cases in 2004, we estimate the following figures:

year	population	# of homicides	#/100,000	# unsolved
1940	76,212,168	4,560	6	1,705
1990	248,709,873	24,800	10	9,275
2000	281,421,906	20,232	7.2	7,566

According to current FBI statistics, over a third of all murder cases go unsolved. The East Chop murder is listed as unsolved, even though the preponderance of evidence points to Harold Tracy. Because he was indicted, but never tried, and the charges were nol-prossed, the case is still considered open.

All evidence pointed to Harold Tracy as the suspect, yet other than the *Vineyard Gazette* and trial transcript, I had virtually no background data on our man. So I set out to find him. Talks with retired FBI agents led to a composite of suggestions on how to track him down. Agents recommended I research birth, death and court records and intimated a personal visit to his hometown could be productive.

"Start with Vanceburg, Kentucky, to get an exact date of birth," suggested the first agent. "The state registry of vital statistics is in Frankfort. Many of the records are now on computer. Go to Kentucky state government. It's amazing how much is out there. Sometimes it's easy, other times it's tedious and you can't get your hands on what you need." He cautioned that births were recorded only every five years or so at the start of the twentieth century. "In eastern Kentucky there would be court days, like a country fair, and everyone would come out to have records drawn up, births, marriages and deaths and they'd have an addendum to the records."

Because of poor transportation, Kentucky was broken into 120 counties, second in number only to Texas. Communities were quite insular. Many people never left their hometowns. Dialects of Scottish-English were preserved in isolated pockets. Mining towns offered all the services people needed, from schools to doctors. "Verifying a date of birth can be very difficult," cautioned the agent. "You may have to check the years after, maybe several years afterward."

It was no easier to determine when Harold Tracy died. "Go to Social Security Death Index," said the FBI man, "but it only applies to those who registered for Social Security and made a death claim." Because he rarely worked, it is doubtful Harold Tracy ever registered for Social Security.

"You must have got my number through the Trap Line [available to connect retired FBI agents]," answered a hoarse voice from Kentucky. I explained my goal, and the agent warmed to my search.

"Kentucky was not wired up. My sense is that you should go to the courthouse. Lewis County is the county Vanceburg is located in. Do a hands-on search at the courthouse. Old records may not be computerized. It's like a genealogical study, trying to track down a relative today."

Like his fellow agents, he cautioned patience. "Analysis from data may not be accurate. You have to be aware of that. Can't take the data to the bank." I sensed a smile come down the line. "Go to the courthouse. A little courthouse in Louisville has a bunch of old-timers just sitting around out front, watching people walk across the city square."

A county court clerk had information I sought. Shirley Hinton forwarded copies of an Affidavit of Descent that supplied information on Harold Tracy, his family and land in Vanceburg. It was rewarding.

The agent suggested we try the Freedom of Information Act with the FBI and "go for Interstate Transport of a Stolen Motor Vehicle, a DIRE case," to track down the carjacking incident that sent Tracy to the federal penitentiary. The agent advised, "Vital statistics may not be available to the general public. Some records are more restrictive or may have been destroyed or you may get lucky." Federal penitentiaries, from Lewisburg to Pendleton, did not furnish records on Tracy's prison terms.

The next agent said, "Fellow must have had relatives with the same name. Get a lead. Get into it. It's fun." It was.

"If nothing else, get the flavor of the area. Not much going on. Shoeshine parlor still there. Blacksmith shop. Check it all out. Find the house he was born in, his school, his parents' graves. Read the Vanceburg newspaper."

So I boarded a plane to Kentucky and did what the agent suggested, dining with local historian Dr. William Talley and talking up my search with everyone from the proprietor of the Victorian Rose restaurant to a resident of the Golden Living nursing home. I was advised to "try to locate the property he inherited at Black Oak Bottom. In Vanceburg, someone must know about it." I found the site of Tracy's house, his parents' graves, the house he was born in and the school he attended. On a side note, I sought information on Tracy's sister's family in Hammond, Indiana, but to no avail.

I visited the Lewis County Historical Society and spoke with Betty Caseman, who supplied a key letter that gave birth and death dates.[26] At the end of the day I felt I knew a good deal more about my suspect and his colorful past.

While I couldn't justify all that went wrong in the case, from the murder to the investigation, through the incarceration to the prosecution, I felt better able to make sense of the situation as it was handled by various officials and officers in that long-ago era of 1940.

EPILOGUE

As I drive my school bus along the lazy, leafy lanes of Lambert's Cove and up Indian Hill on Martha's Vineyard, I sense a connection with that sylvan site on East Chop in the long-ago summer of 1940. Some of my students may well be descended from players of that era.

That summer was a last gasp of normalcy before the war. Yet tranquility was tossed asunder by the brutal rape and grisly murder. An innocent man was charged and then set free, and no one was ever brought to trial again. The murder of Mrs. Smith was washed aside by the stream of blood from the war.

The impact of the world war on this case cannot be ignored. While Crossley and Stokes framed charges against Huntingdon, the Nazis bombed Britain. In response, the United States geared up with a draft. By the time Tracy was caught after his jailbreak, the United States was engaged in war on two fronts. The three-year-old murder was eclipsed by the savagery of Hitler. By 1946, after Crossley was forced out of office, Vineyarders resolved the case on their own. The murder faded into an isolated prewar memory.

It was time to move on. People on the Vineyard reverted to that naive innocence that thrives today, with houses unlocked, keys in car ignitions and a basic trust in one another, at least in the off-season when we recognize most people we encounter.

The murder assumed the role of a storied rumor or a blurry rumination, buried in a long lost past. The innocent serenity that accompanies the natural beauty of the island and the sense of security in our isolated outpost is as strong today as it was in the days before Harold Tracy and Huntingdon Rice hogged the headlines.

NOTES

CHAPTER TWO

1. Bob Penney of Oak Bluffs recalled that his parents ran the Dinette, a little restaurant like Linda Jeans on Circuit Avenue. A roast beef dinner cost ninety-nine cents. For years, the cook was Mabel Bracy. In return for placing a weekly poster from the playhouse in the window, Phidelah gave Bob's parents two free tickets to the theatre each week. "I used to go with my mother. She thought it was part of my education. We saw *Uncle Tom's Cabin*, *The Moon is Blue* and *Seven Keys to Baldpate*."

Billy Norton recalls, "The Rice Playhouse was up on Brewster Avenue. It was a big old building, very popular with the summer people. They thought the natives didn't have the culture. We were slower, more laid back. There was a definite split back then between the summer people, the tourists and the natives."

Adelaide Bangs Urquhart remembered the playhouse. "Students often found little spots in the surrounding woods to practice Voice exercises, and perhaps a bit of repertoire."

Dean Denniston added to the image. "I used to hear voices in the woods. Students would walk in the woods and recite their lines."

2. Barbara Hoyle's brother Merrill acted in *Treasure Island* at the playhouse. Nancy Young remembers Phidelah Rice, with his impressive appearance, being very involved in the productions of the Children's Theatre. Mary Lib Peterson recalled, "The Rice Playhouse was the best place to go. We all belonged to it, to the children's theatre. East Chop was quiet, few automobiles, but it's all different, it's changed."

3. Years later the Houghs put their conservation ideals to practical purpose. Their brochure reads,

> *Sheriff's Meadow Foundation was chartered in 1959 by Henry Beetle Hough, longtime editor of the* Vineyard Gazette *and ardent conservation spokesman. He wished to protect natural areas "to serve as living museums." Today, this Island-based land trust has preserved over 2600 acres in acquisition and conservation restrictions.*
>
> *Sheriff's Meadow Foundation's mission is to conserve, manage and administer land for wildlife habitat, and to maintain the rural natural character of Martha's Vineyard for present and future generations.*

4. Polly Woolcott Murphy recalled her days working at the *Gazette*. "I was seventeen. We would be sent out on stories and type at home and bring it in the next day. I had nothing to do with reporting the murder. I remember Henry Hough vividly. He was a dear, good man, gentle and sweet, but he could be formidable when he had a cause."

CHAPTER THREE

5.   *July 1, 1940*
       To Ruth Hughes
       Oak Bluffs

> *I want to compliment you on the fine work you did on the Oak Bluffs murder story and for taking it over as competently as you did.*
>
> *We hope you can arrange for pictures and send them down to us on the first boat.*
>
> *Watch for developments in the investigation and for an arrest, if any. Do not permit yourself to be stampeded by baseless reports in the Boston newspapers.*
>
> *Watch the* Vineyard Gazette *closely and if it has anything that we happen to have missed, check it out and send it along.*
>
> *We do not want to be beaten on any angle of this story and we are counting on you to continue the fine work that you did Sunday and Monday.*
>
> > *Charles Lewin*
> > *Editor in Chief*
> > The Standard Times—Morning Mercury
> > *New Bedford*

It is curious that the front page of the *New Bedford Standard Times* for July 1, 1940, is missing, although page two, printed on the back, is safely secure on microfilm at both the New Bedford Public Library and the campus of the University of Massachusetts in Dartmouth, a repository for the entire *New Bedford Standard Times*. Even the office of the *Standard Times* can only produce the *Morning Mercury* front page for July 1, not the *Standard Times*.

6. Louise Pearce of Oak Bluffs, twenty years old at the time, recalled that the murder shocked the community. "It was not openly discussed," she recounted sixty years later. "We all knew about it and read about it, but it was hush-hush."

Mrs. Charles Cooper recalled, "An elderly woman was killed. I was seventeen and lived on East Chop. We used to talk about it on the beach. Isn't it terrible! They thought it was robbery."

Stuart Bangs remembered when he first heard of the murder. "I'd been on a boat to Cuttyhunk that day and I came back and someone on the dock hollered there'd been a murder. Now that was a big deal on Martha's Vineyard. I remember it distinctly."

Phyllis Meras recalled, "I remember that night. My brother and I walked up East Chop Drive past the Beach Club and past the dormitory on our way home from the movies. It was the night the murder was going on. The next day we learned that a murder was committed there. We lived on Monroe Street at the time, off Brewster, behind the tennis courts. The murder was the talk of the island. I was eight or nine, so my recollection is not that good."

She went on. "We used to walk through the Downs, which was the area across from the dormitory, where they said a bundle of clothes was found after the murder. We used to pick blueberries, huckleberries and boxberries there. There was a sandy area with tiger lilies."

Mary Lib Peterson summered on East Chop from the 1930s to the 1980s. "We didn't hear a thing that night. Police with flashlights went running through the yards to locate the criminal. After that horrible thing, parents said now you have to be careful and we locked our doors even when we went down to the beach. We kept it quiet as we didn't want to alarm the summer visitors."

Constance Long Spaulding remembered, "I had a portable radio and we were at the dock in Woods Hole. I put it on while we waited for the boat and that's when I heard what happened for the first time." Connie was only fifteen, en route to the Vineyard to visit her grandmother that summer. "It was a great scandal. Great deal of questions about who did it and why. I think they indicated that a man who ran the school did it."

Billy Norton recalled, "I was about twelve at the time. First time we had a murder right here in Oak Bluffs." He went on, "We figured it was a summer people's problem and would go away by Labor Day. Now I'm older, but that's the attitude back then."

7. "We were asked to keep the Rice School secretary over night as she was so frightened by the murder. Apparently Huntingdon had said something to her, and that got her scared. That's when we lived on Maple Avenue, the middle bungalow." Ruth Hughes remembered this episode in 2002 and confirmed it in 2007.

8. Henry Hough reported the police interrogation of Huntingdon Rice in his book, *Once More the Thunderer*:

> *The detectives closed in. "Now you wrote that letter on July 1st, is that right?"*
> *"Yes, sir."*
> *"And you mailed that letter after you got the information?"*
> *"I must have."*
> *"Now, you look at the mailing stamp."*
> *"I see the mailing stamp."*
> *"Read it."*
> *"It says 'June 30th,' I think. That is what it says, '11 a.m., June 30th.'"*
> *"Read the back of it, when it was received in New York."*
> *"July 1st, 6:30 a.m."*
> *"Now, if you can explain that, you can walk right out of here."*
> *"Well...of course I either made the mistake..."*
> *"Just a minute," broke in Captain [Stokes]. "You explain that without any ceremony, you explain that as glibly as you have explained everything else here today, and you can walk right out of here. Can you explain it?"*
> *"How could anyone explain a thing like that? I don't know. All I know is that I never knew anything about it until Monday when my sister told me on the porch."*
> *"You explain why you wrote that letter and dated it July 1st, and it has a mailing stamp on it when you mailed it as of June 30th, when you contend you knew nothing about this until Monday, and you date this July 1st. Now you explain it if you can."*
> *"Well, I don't know..."*
> [Rice] *examined the letter, looked at it closely, looked at the envelope. There was a long pause, sighs. He took out a pocket magnifier and examined the postmark with care. He peered around the room, glanced up, closed his eyes, and let his head drop.*
> *"I may term it a grimace, if I may," testified the stenographer later. "Perspiration started on his forehead, began to trickle down. I noticed a flush on his right cheek, more than on the left, that flared up red. There*

was no answer. This continued for about, I should say, ten minutes. Then he started an answer."

"Well, I know I am guilt—I am innocent sir. I know I never knew anything about it until my sister told me."

CHAPTER FIVE

9. Letter written by Harold Tracy to Marjorie Massow, reprinted in *Once More the Thunderer* by Henry Hough.

Dearest: I once told you that your happiness meant more to me than anything in the world, and if what I have done has hurt you, it may ease the hurt a little to know why I have taken this way out.

It's not because I'm guilty of the beastly crime of which they suspect me—God, I could never have done that—but because of a ghost of my past which is bound to be resurrected by this investigation—a ghost which I have prayed to God would never be disturbed again.

I was starved for happiness and the right to live as other men do. Should I ever have been able to win your love, you would never have had cause to regret it. Some day they'll find the beast and then he will be twice a murderer, because my blood will be on his hands in addition to that of that poor old lady.

You remember telling me you were still a virgin—and my telling you that I wouldn't rob you of your virginity even should you request it—much less invite it. I loved and respected you too much for that, as I've always respected all women…Now they're trying to prove that I visited Sumner that night with the intention of violating your chastity…And so, not because of that crime, but because of my past—because I've lost you forever, I'm taking this way out.

I go, with your image on my heart, and your name on my lips.

10. It was later revealed that prominent actress Katharine Cornell, of Vineyard Haven, loaned the Rice Playhouse $200 to keep it viable through that summer season of 1940.

CHAPTER SIX

11. When I learned the trial transcript was housed at the Martha's Vineyard Museum, I requested it. Mysteriously, it took a three-week search to locate the missing volume, which had apparently been misfiled by a summer intern. A similar situation occurred in the courthouse, where letters and evidence reviewed once were not found on later requests.

12. Stuart Bangs recalled, "Keatings and the post office were both on Circuit Avenue. I felt they did a better job with the mail back then than they do now. They didn't have as many people and service. Now we have to send our mail to Providence to use the letter sorting machines."

Then the mail traveled by train, was sorted on the train and was delivered more promptly by train. Metropolitan areas, and sites close to rail service, benefitted. Mail to remote regions, however, took much longer to deliver.

With today's mail, as Mr. Bangs points out, the intent is to maximize regional postal centers. Island mail is picked up once a day and goes through Providence, Cape Cod or Boston, depending on the day's volume. It takes as long to send a letter from Oak Bluffs to San Francisco as it does to New York. Or to Vineyard Haven.

13. Christian Scientists believe healing comes from Jesus, not through medicine or physicians. Mrs. White's correspondence with Huntingdon was designed to reaffirm the teachings of Jesus to help heal his medical issues.

From *Christian Science, Science and Health with Key to the Scriptures*, by Mary Baker Eddy: "Christian Scientists believe in one supreme God, whose intent is to 'do unto us; and to be merciful, just, and pure.'"

Mary Baker Eddy discovered Christian Science in 1866 when she was healed from a serious spinal injury after suffering years of poor health. She set about to discover how she cured herself.

Without the aid of medicine, Miss Eddy began to heal people. She put her thoughts on paper and composed a textbook in 1875 entitled *Christian Science, Science and Health with Key to the Scriptures*.

"After my discovery of Christian Science," she wrote, "I healed consumption in its last stages, malignant diphtheria and physically restored sight to the blind, hearing to the deaf, speech to the dumb, and have made the lame walk." She felt she furthered the tradition of Jesus in the healing he performed.

The essence of Christian Science is that God is good and has made all things like him. Existence, Christian Scientists believe, is spiritual rather than material. Prayer is not a request for redemption or assistance but a means to learn more about the spirituality of God. Healthcare results from spiritual healing, not medicine or surgery, according to Christian Science doctrine.

Nearly half a million adherents of Christian Science abide by the text Mary Baker Eddy wrote more than a century ago. The Rice family were strong believers in Christian Science. The family was instrumental in developing the church on New York Avenue in Oak Bluffs. Classes at the school featured elements of Christian Science, such as Bible reading.

Huntingdon gained confidence in his personal and physical struggles through the practitioner Edna White. When Phidelah fell ill in the spring of 1940, no medical intervention was sought. In later years, Elizabeth practiced the faith in her home in Boston. Eschewing medical treatment, the Rices practiced Christian Science for years.

14. Mrs. White destroyed the letter dated June 30, but saved the envelope from that letter. She saved the letter dated July 1, which included the damning postscript, but lost the envelope. The police put the July 1 letter in the June 30 envelope, and considered that sufficient evidence to compel Huntingdon to confess. He refused.

CHAPTER SEVEN

15. Hough recounted his efforts in his tome, *Once More the Thunderer*:

> *Nevertheless, the trial had spread upon public record certain evidence that needed more attention than it had yet received. We were afraid the district attorney would drop everything, as the easiest way out, and therefore it was up to the* Gazette *to force the issue, and force it we did. We had no desire to convict* [Tracy] *in advance, but we wanted the murder solved if it could be solved by any effort humanly possible.*

16. On the Rice Playhouse: "The theatre was closed during the war and because of the murder," according to Elizabeth Suppes of Vineyard Haven, who ran a small inn with a dining room on the site. "I rented the dormitory [Sumner Hall] and the whole theatre where the students slept and ate. The murder took place on the second floor. The rooms were small, single rooms that overlooked the ocean." Suppes rented the Hall from 1946 to 1950.

17. Susan Canha is the daughter of Carolee, granddaughter of Phidelah and Elizabeth Rice, and grandniece of Ralph Huntingdon Rice. She lives on Martha's Vineyard.

> *My mother's name was Carolee Rice Leathe, and I am Susan Leathe Canha. We grew up with no knowledge of the murder. Never knew anything had taken place. Mother did mention it briefly, but it was very upsetting to her because of the effect it had on her parents.*
>
> *I went to my grandmother's home in Boston during school vacations. She was a true Christian Scientist. She was a teacher, and when I visited I had to be quiet when she had a student with her. She lived near the Charles River in Boston.*
>
> *Mother used to summer in New Hampshire. When my grandmother sold the East Chop house, we rented a place when we came to the Vineyard in the mid-1950s.*
>
> *Mother would get upset when someone from the era passed away and the papers identified the person as connected to the Rice murder. At least*

Henry Beetle Hough kept that reference out of the Gazette. *She never mentioned the murder around her children, never spoke of it, never wanted to discuss it.*

When I moved back to the island, I would mention that my grandparents had the Rice Playhouse, kind of to brag. The older people would remember going to see plays, then someone would say someone was murdered there, but I didn't want to ask my mother about it. She was a very private person.

When we [Susan and her two cousins] *were in our thirties and forties we would sneak over to the Oak Bluffs library and read up on the trial. My cousin was the mastermind with the microfiche and once we ran into my mother at the library and had to make up an excuse as to why we were there!*

The Rice School had so much to offer. It's a shame one incident brought about its end. Mother knew a lot of the famous actors and actresses who performed at the Playhouse. Growing up, I knew about [the playhouse] *in my teen years.*

18. A 1954 realtor's notebook describes the theatre and West Cottage for sale or rent for $800; no water or electricity included. Elizabeth Rice also offered the Rice Cottage, which featured a large living room, fireplace, dining room, enclosed and screened porches, kitchen, gas range and electric icebox, five bedrooms, one bath, tower room and extra toilet. The asking price was $6,500 to buy or $450 per month to rent, $700 in season.

CHAPTER EIGHT

19. Catherine King (ninety-three) of Vanceburg clearly recalled Harold Tracy from her youth. "He was tall and slender," she said with a twinkle in her eye.

She was upset by the desecration of the cemetery. "He had the name on it," she said, and implied he was involved in other vandalism. Mrs. King ran the King and Sullivan Liquor Store on Second Street for forty years, and may have sold alcohol to Harold Tracy.

Margaret Wilson (ninety-one) at Golden Living recalled Tracy "was sent up for something. He wasn't around." She was too polite to share the details.

Roy Chinn was raised near the Tracy home in Black Oak Bottom. He recalled the Tracys kept dogs in their home. Chinn recalled William Tracy would drive his tractor into town on Saturday.

20. Bill T. Clark of Vanceburg, Kentucky, has a play program from a play entitled *The Patsy*, which was released in 1928 as a movie that starred Marie Dressler and Marion Davies. Bill Clark says, "Harold Tracy did indeed

appear in the cast, playing the part of one 'Billy Caldwell.' My mother, Kathryn Clark, played the part of 'Patricia Harrington,' the character which gave the play its name." A photograph of the cast includes Harold Tracy. Mr. Clark says he "was indeed in this play, given on Thursday evening, March 29, 1928."

21. The story of Tracy's one-time girlfriend, Marjorie Massow, led deep into a California canyon. In 1947, Marjorie, a second-rate actress under the assumed name of Madge Meredith, hired three thugs to beat up her former business manager and his bodyguard in a deserted gulch outside Hollywood. She was convicted and sentenced to five years at Tehachapi prison, southeast of Bakersfield, but no records of her incarceration are available. The current population of the facility is male. And there the trail of this once promising ingénue grows cold.

22.   *Black Oak Bottom is much different now than it was in the '30s, '40s and '50s. Much of the land has been taken for roads and factories. I remember the house where the Tracys lived. It was a big two-story house, built with a long room [one story] in the back. The house burned sometime between 1947 and 1951. A smaller house was built in its place. The lady who lives on the property now said the property went to the railroad at one time. The original houses are not there. Two other newer houses have been built there. They were recently moved back for the road to be widened.*

This was contributed by Joan Godfrey of Vanceburg, Kentucky, a retired teacher who volunteers at the Lewis County Historical Society.

23. Dr. William Talley of Vanceburg reported, "Mrs. Shirley Hinton, the [Lewis] county court clerk, says she met Mr. Tracy about 1960 when he came to the courthouse to deal with settlement with the Laney family. Mrs. Hinton recalled Tracy as a tall, thin, well-dressed, nice-looking man."

When we spoke with Mrs. Hinton, she added, "He was a smart cookie. I can see him coming in the front door. He was tall, held his shoulders back. I can picture him. A fine looking man." She considered his intent to sell the family homestead. "He thought it was time to get out of town and sold."

Dr. Talley sent out an appeal for more information on Harold Tracy in October 2007 on "Talley's History Page," a weekly column he contributes to the *Lewis County Herald*.

Mr. Talley wrote,

   Harold Tracy was interested in the theater as early as his boyhood days when he took part in theatrical productions in Vanceburg. Mrs. Shirley Hinton and Mrs. Catherine King have been helpful in researching Mr.

Tracy but we have come to a "dead end" and hope someone can volunteer some information to Mr. Dresser. Incidentally, it is of interest that Harold Tracy was closely related to the late William C. Dugan.

CHAPTER NINE

24. The old jail, with just two cells, stood to the left of the courthouse, behind the World War II memorial. The dip in the ground is where the well was. In 1940, the red brick courthouse was square; the back ell was added in 1956 to house court offices.

25. In 1975, District Attorney Philip Rollins split the Southern District into two sections: Cape Cod and the islands, the responsibility of Michael O'Keefe and Bristol County, run by District Attorney C. Samuel Sutter. Archives on District Attorney William Crossley would be housed in Bristol County, but no information was available.

26. Letter to Bill Dugan, editor of the *Lewis County Herald*:

March 2, 1972
Dear Bill:

Harold Thomas Tracy was born on May 17th 1903 (in the Grant McDaniel—now Ernest Lee—dwelling in Vanceburg) and passed away in Hammond, Indiana on Aug. 28th 1964. He died of emphysema, a lung condition he had for a number of years.

He was married only once to my knowledge and divorced when I was very young. I think he had one daughter, but I never saw her, only remember slightly. Only my mother, my two sisters, one brother, and myself survived him. He is buried close to my mother in Elmwood Cemetery, Hammond, Ind.

Sorry you didn't know about his death—had I known more of his friends, I could have passed on the word to you. He was a brilliant man—if only he had taken advantage of his intelligence—he could have been setting on East [sic] Street all those years.

I come to visit my grandparents' graves in Black Oak every couple of years. Next time I will stop and see you. Tell my friend Dr. Bertram [Sr.] hello from me when you see him. He isn't quite sure he remembers me.

Sincerely
Dorothy Hartog
[Harold Tracy's niece]

156

BIBLIOGRAPHY

It was a treat to inhabit the era of 1940. From poring over dozens of yellowed *Gazettes*, through a precise perusal of the trial transcript, to interviews with old-timers and enthusiastic researchers, it's been a great journey.

My two primary sources of research for this book were the morgue of the *Vineyard Gazette* and the trial transcript housed at the Martha's Vineyard Museum. My sincere gratitude to Joe Pitt of the *Gazette* and Matthew Stackpole of the Museum.

Baden, Dr. Michael, and Marion Roach. *Dead Reckoning*. New York: Simon & Schuster, 2001.

Brownmiller, Susan. *Against Our Will: Men, Women and Rape*. New York: Simon and Schuster, 1975.

Clayton, Tim, and Phil Craig. *Finest Hour: Battle of Britain*. New York: Simon & Schuster, 1999.

Hough, Henry Beetle. *Once More the Thunderer*. Topeka, KS: Washburn Press, 1950.

Larson, Erik. *The Devil in the White City*. New York: Random House, 2003.

Meras, Phyllis. *Country Editor Henry Beetle Hough and the* Vineyard Gazette. Martha's Vineyard: Images from the Past and the Martha's Vineyard Historical Society, 2006.

ABOUT THE AUTHOR

After a stint as an elementary schoolteacher and a couple of decades as a nursing home administrator, Tom Dresser stepped back and realized he wanted to write. Besides freelance contributions to the local press, he has also self-published five booklets based on favorite New England haunts:

Dogtown, A Village Lost in Time (1995)
Beyond Bar Harbor (1996)
It Happened in Haverhill (1997)
Looking at Lawrence (1998)
Tommy's Tour of the Vineyard (2005)

On a personal note, he attended his thirtieth high school reunion and ran into a woman who sat beside him way back when. She lived on Martha's Vineyard, invited him down for a weekend and the rest, as they say, is history! Tom has two grown daughters, both in education. Amy Dresser Held works in Los Angeles, and Jill Dresser teaches in New Orleans. He also has three stepchildren—Jeremy Jones, Jennifer Smyth and Christopher Jones—and two granddaughters, Shealyn Smyth and Molly Rose Held.

Visit us at
www.historypress.net